WHEREVER YOU GO

WHEREVER YOU GO

A Guide to Mindful, Sustainable, and Life-Changing Travel

DANIEL HOUGHTON

TILLER PRESS

New York London Toronto Sydney New Delhi

TILLER PRESS

Tiller Press
An Imprint of Simon & Schuster, Inc.
1230 Avenue of the Americas
New York, NY 10020

First Tiller Press hardcover edition November 2019

TILLER PRESS and colophon are trademarks of Simon & Schuster, Inc.

For information about special discounts for bulk purchases, please contact Simon &
Schuster Special Sales at 1-866-506-1949 or business@simonandschuster.com.

The Simon & Schuster Speakers Bureau can bring authors to your live event. For
more information or to book an event, contact the Simon & Schuster Speakers
Bureau at 1-866-248-3049 or visit our website at www.simonspeakers.com.

Manufactured in the United States of America

10 9 8 7 6 5 4 3 2 1

Library of Congress Control Number: 2019947677

ISBN 978-1-9821-3158-6
ISBN 978-1-9821-3159-3 (ebook)

5:45 a.m., March 4, 2019

It's cold as can be outside in Nashville, Tennessee. I've just walked into the hospital to spend the day with my mom and dad at Vanderbilt University Medical Center.

My father, Dan Houghton, is seventy-two years old. He was born in 1946 in Boston, the third of seven children. Today we are at Vanderbilt as a family for a surgery that's scheduled for him.

Eight months ago, he was diagnosed with stage four cancer. It was a total surprise when it happened, and he rushed to the emergency room after not feeling right for several days. I was in Mexico for work, and my mom was in Kentucky visiting her mother. He was all alone, and the last thing we heard from him that day was when he called my cell phone to tell me they were going to operate; he would call when he could.

Fast-forward eight months and here we are, sitting in the waiting room watching a six-digit number scroll across a screen with a hundred other numbers, telling us the status of his six-hour surgery.

Mom and I are posted up at a desk near the back wall with our phones plugged in, just waiting. I spent the morning making grammatical edits to this book, and Mom was pretty busy keeping family members updated with text messages and phone calls.

The surgery is to reverse a procedure they did during the first emergency surgery he had eight months before. A little over a month ago, they declared him cancer-free, a real miracle given the severity of his original diagnosis.

A few days earlier, I was here with him for pre-operation procedures, and that was enough for me to remember just how much I hate the hospital. People crying in the elevators, doctors trying to explain things to patients as methodically as possible.

Mom gets a text on her phone telling us to see the front desk in the waiting room area, and we walk over. His surgery started about 7 a.m., and it was approaching 12:30, so we were expecting an update any minute.

The doctor sits Mom and my aunt Sally and me down in the corner of the waiting room with a sign overhead that reads "Doctor-Patient Consultation Area." She introduces herself and begins to walk us through the surgery she has just completed minutes before.

At first, it sounds like things are going great. I start to notice a shift in her voice, and then she says: "Unfortunately, we have some unexpected results." They have found more cancer.

More chemo would follow, but we knew he had the best team of oncology specialists at Vanderbilt. There is always hope.

Mom asked some tough questions, and the answers hit me like a ton of bricks. I have been through many emotional roller coasters with Dad's health in the last year, but none so severe and brutal as this five-minute explanation.

"Does he know yet?" Mom asks.

"No, and you don't have to tell him. I can tell him with you both in the room," the surgeon says.

Twenty minutes later, Mom and I are allowed to go up to recovery to see him. He is awake and has an instant smile on his face when he sees me first. "Where's my bride?" he asks me.

"She's right here," I say.

He sees Mom and takes a breath, and then he starts crying. I've never seen my dad cry, and I'm thirty years old. We are pretty close, and have been through our fair share of lousy shit over the years.

"Why are you crying, honey?" Mom asks him.

"It's finally over," he says.

My heart sinks, and I almost throw up. I knew we were going to have to break the news to him. We let him calm down a little bit, and he starts asking us how things have gone. We tell him they went well. Then Mom speaks up and says, "They did find a few more spots." He just looks at us with a blank stare. He is still pretty drugged up from the anesthesia, but it is painfully clear he knows exactly what we are saying.

I take over for Mom, and explain what the surgeon told us. He stares off into the distance for several minutes, listening, and then says: "I knew it was too good to be true."

I'm telling this story because of a few reasons. Obviously, my dad is a huge part of my life, and this has been a horrific year for our family, but something happened later that day that made me realize I wanted this to be a part of this book.

One of Mom and Dad's longtime friends, Diane, whom they had not seen in decades, was in Nashville on a layover. She and Mom were flight attendants together at Delta, and she had picked up a Nashville trip to see them both.

I'm not sure Dad had seen her in twenty years, but I quickly learned that Diane was there the day my mom and dad met in the eighties, and was a part of their friend group from the very beginning of their relationship.

My dad is a storyteller, so as soon as we were moved from recovery and taken to a room, visitors were allowed, and Diane came up to say hi. Dad was telling the doctors to hurry up, because we had friends visiting that he hadn't seen in twenty years.

"Well, you haven't changed a bit," Diane said when she first saw my dad.

"Well, the outfit is a little different," he said, gesturing to his hospital gown.

They spent the next hour sharing stories from thirty years ago. I wasn't paying attention at first, but then I realized they were all travel stories.

They talked about trips they had all taken, places they had skied, people they had met, remembered, and forgotten. Dad has traveled extensively throughout his life and, as you will read in the pages that follow, spent endless amounts of time as a family traveling together.

After this went on for a while, the room got quiet. Then Dad said, "I always knew, when I was laying in a hospital bed or nursing home one day, I'm not going to have a frown on my face from what I didn't do, I'm going to have a smile on my face remembering the things I did."

This book is dedicated to my dad, Daniel Matthew Houghton. Thank you for loving Mom, Kate, and me, and raising me to be the person I am today. For everyone else that's reading this, hug your loved ones. You never know how much time you have left. I love you, Dad.

—Daniel

CONTENTS

AUTHOR'S NOTE

When I set out to write this book, I was so excited to explain the endless ways in which travel changes us for the better. I made list upon list of examples and reasons why I so passionately believe that travel can change the world.

These examples were mostly stories from friends and colleagues that reinforced everything I was writing about. I quickly realized I couldn't convince any of you on my own.

I wanted you to hear it straight from some of the most inspiring people I've ever met or had the chance to speak with. It takes more than one perspective to convey the magical experiences that will happen to you when you hit the road.

With that in mind, I created a new list: one filled with people that I knew could get the point across far better than my own stories and experiences. I've had the pleasure of speaking with some of the most inspiring travelers of our time for this book, and I'm honored to share them with you. They have been edited for clarity and in some cases condensed, but the spirit of each is intact.

Most of the people I wound up with on my dream list of interviews I didn't know or have any connection to. I randomly contacted almost everyone in this book, by various means—tweets to their public profiles, guessing at email addresses, and begging their PR agents or representatives to respond. Fortunately, most everyone likes to share a good travel story.

Some of these people are famous, and you will know them well. Many of them are unknown, but have stories and experiences that match anything you will hear from a celebrity.

From Sir Richard Branson's lifelong mission to explore the world (and space) to Kevan Chandler's story of seeing Europe for the first time only because his friends carried him around in a homemade backpack, I hope these stories inspire you to get out and see everything the world has to offer.

There are tales of travels on submarines and Air Force One; of what it's like to captain a megayacht for a reality show or to sail alone around the world at the tender age of sixteen.

What ties the stories all together is their tellers' relentless drive to learn and experience as much as they can in the one life we all have to live. I hope they make you laugh, cry, and pull out your credit card to book a ticket.

Best,
Daniel

WHY TRAVEL MATTERS

Travel—verb: make a journey, typically of some length or abroad.

There's a scene from the 2000 film *The Beach*, starring a young Leonardo DiCaprio, that always comes to mind when I think about what the real definition of the word "travel" is.

In the scene, DiCaprio's character, Richard, has just taken an eighteen-hour transoceanic flight to Bangkok, and he's wandering the streets looking for a place to sleep. As he makes his way into a run-down hostel filled with backpackers from around the world, he's talking to you, the viewer, about the point of travel.

He talks about coming on this trip perhaps because he was looking for something "more beautiful, more exciting, and maybe even something more dangerous" than his life back home.

"Like every tourist, you want your trip to be safe, just like America. The only downer is, everyone's got the same idea. We all travel thousands of miles away just to watch TV and check into somewhere with all the comforts of home. And you gotta ask yourself . . . What is the point of that?"

An excellent question. What is the point of that? What does travel mean to you? Is it sitting on a beach without a care in the world, like Richard? Is it an adventure without much of a plan that you're dying to experience? Could it be a meticulously planned, schedule-driven checklist that you've been researching for months? Or is travel just something that you dream about and know you want to do, but you don't really ever take the time or money to actually get off your ass and go?

Since we are going to be spending some time together throughout this book, I'll give you a quick background on what travel means to me. And why I wanted to write this book, and change your mind on what travel *can* be for the world we live in.

I've been traveling most of my life. My parents worked on planes their entire lives, Dad as a mechanic and Mom as a flight attendant. They met while working for Delta Air Lines, living in different cities. Dad had relocated to Atlanta from Boston, where he grew up, after Delta bought Northeast Airlines in 1972, and Mom was living in Fort Lauderdale, Florida. After a six-month romance in 1985, they married and settled down in Fayetteville, Georgia, a nice, growing suburb just outside Atlanta—only thirteen miles from the busiest airport on earth, Hartsfield-Jackson Atlanta International.

I'm having a hard time remembering exactly when in elementary school this happened, but at some point, we had to write a paper about our favorite place. You can predict the answers kids wrote down: Disney World. The Mall. The Movies. The Beach. Home.

I wrote about the only place that I ever wanted to spend time. The airport.

The airport, to me, was all of the other kids' answers rolled into one. Not only did it have a mall inside, but the planes also had movies and would fly you to Orlando if you asked. No contest!

One of the big perks of having airline parents was "free tickets." I put that in quotes because my dad used to joke with people that those "free tickets" were like a gift from hell. It was actually pretty close to the furthest thing from a free ticket you could imagine. Here's how it worked:

Airline employees had free pass privileges to fly on the airline that they work for. Luckily for me, Delta was (and still is) the largest airline in the world (by market capitalization), and was flying to the most destinations at the time. Unfortunately, your ability to actually get on any given flight depended on a matrix of how many seats were unsold and how many years you had worked for the airline. Basically, you had the right to show up to the airport and stand by in case there were empty seats, either because they went unsold or because someone missed their connecting flight or just failed to show up.

After all the paying passengers boarded the flight, the counter would start to call a list of names in order of available seats, starting with the most senior employee. I don't think we ever paid for a single ticket when I was growing up; we just learned the system and tried our best to work it.

This method definitely had its downsides. Imagine planning a family ski trip, getting the kids all excited, packing your bags, driving to the airport, turning up to the gate, watching the plane board, and then finding out, despite having checked the records in advance to ensure there were twenty-two empty seats to Salt Lake City, that the flight has been "oversold." Or watching a group of people from a connecting flight running up to the gate at the last minute, dragging their luggage, to take *your ticket* away—and then watching the door to the jetway close and lock.

———

As I got older and my parents gained seniority, I got more adventurous with my travels. College was a sweet spot, because although Dad was retired, Mom was nearing thirty-five years of employment with Delta. I could turn up to nearly any flight, at least until I turned twenty-three, and almost always be at the top of the standby list. I took free flights to Africa, South America, and Europe, as well as countless trips around the United States.

I particularly remember one last-minute jaunt to Africa. My college classmate Shane Noem was going with his mom and dad down to Johannesburg for the summer. (Shane grew up on a farm, so he was definitely not the rich city boy this story makes him sound like.) His younger brother had just been admitted to the Air Force Academy and couldn't make the family trip they had been planning for a year.

We were talking one day over iChat while I was at my summer internship at Fort Knox. He jokingly said, "You should come since Derek can't make it," and I said something to the effect of "Don't tempt me, I can fly for free anywhere Delta Air Lines goes."

Two weeks later I was on a fifteen-hour, thirty-five-minute, one-layover flight to Johannesburg. I was eighteen years old and alone. I'm still not sure what my parents were thinking letting me go, but I boarded the flight and even got a free upgrade to first class (thanks, Mom!).

I spent the next three weeks living—not traveling—in South Africa. Shane's dad was there for work, so we lived in a house that was part of a large compound several hours outside of Johannesburg. Shane and I were both studying to be photographers, so we spent most of our time begging our way onto safari trips that were going out so we could see the wildlife. Some days we just got dropped off in a tree house to sit for hours on end, without a cell phone or anything other than a friendly assurance that "we will be back to get you in a few hours."

Every year that passed felt like time slipping away on my free ticket to the world. Mom was getting close to retirement, and I would soon be too old to use my privileges. I spent most of my time in college classes trying to figure out how I could keep traveling after the ride was over.

I'll fast-forward several years to when I was twenty-four and found myself running one of the world's most famous travel companies, Lonely Planet. I'll explain the how and why of that in the next chapter, but to my great and unexpected joy, I had made it. I was traveling for a living.

Running the world's largest travel publisher, as you can imagine, involves quite a lot of travel. We had twelve offices across four continents. I was regularly spending time in Europe, Aus-

5

tralia, India, and China. My first full year as CEO I did 350,000 miles. In one particularly busy two-week stretch, I flew around the world three different times, in opposite directions.

I was taking around two hundred flights a year, mostly international, and only spending two or three days in the places I was visiting. My childhood fascination with the airport had never faded.

To reference another movie, recall *Up in the Air*, the 2009 comedy-drama about George Clooney's constant-travel job for a company that helped other companies downsize. This movie hit particularly close to home for a lot of reasons, including the fact that the first thing I had to do at Lonely Planet was significantly restructure the business, which left a lot of good people without jobs.

There's a scene in the movie where Clooney's character describes his life, and job, fondly. "All the things you probably hate about traveling—the recycled air, the artificial lighting, the digital juice dispensers, the cheap sushi—are warm reminders that I'm home." I've never agreed with anything more.

Richard Branson
"76 Near-Death Experiences"

Sir Richard Branson, best known as the founder of the Virgin Group, has made a life out of avoiding death while traveling. From a solo journey across the Atlantic Ocean in a hot-air balloon to leading the charge to take humanity into space, Richard has shown no signs of slowing down, even at sixty-eight. He's been to all seven continents and is continually challenging himself to explore new places and push boundaries.

Daniel Houghton: How have your travels changed you as a person?
Richard Branson: Visiting new places and meeting new people has opened my mind in many ways—and presented so many opportunities. Mark Twain summed it up nicely when he said: "Travel is fatal to prejudice, bigotry, and narrow-mindedness." When you meet so many different people from different cultures, you realize that there is more that unites us than divides us. It helped me realize that we can achieve much more when we come together than when we go it alone. It's a big reason why I advocate for diversity and inclusion in the workplace and fight human rights abuses and climate change. We need to look after our planet and our people.

DH: What would you want to tell someone you just met who's never left their home country about why they should travel?
RB: The beauty of life is you can never know everything, and you can always be learning and exploring (being sixty-eight doesn't

7

stop me finding new ways of doing things). If you've never left your home country, then you run the risk of only knowing what you've always known. Progress and innovation come from pushing boundaries, experiencing new things, and always asking questions. Get out of your comfort zone and try something new—I promise you it's an exciting adventure.

DH: Which trip has changed your perspective of the world the most?
RB: There are many moments that have shaped my life and perspective of the world, but my failures have definitely shaped me more than my successes. I've attempted several adventurous world records and was the first person to pilot a hot-air balloon across the Atlantic and the Pacific—but my round-the-world attempt wasn't quite so successful. After accidentally losing most of our fuel, we found ourselves battling gale-force winds above the Pacific Ocean. We had very little hope of rescue if we ditched—we calculated our likelihood of survival at 5 percent. We could either lie down and accept our fate or stay up and try and reach North America. This taught me a really valuable lesson. Never give up!

DH: Share a story of a trip gone horribly wrong, it seems to be a theme. . . .
RB: I have had quite a lot of these—because I love trying new things and experiencing adventure, it often lands me in trouble. In my autobiography, *Finding My Virginity*, I list all seventy-six of my near-death experiences. I had quite a close call with a rock fall last year when I was climbing Mont Blanc for the Virgin Strive Challenge, where we cycle, sea kayak, hike, and climb

two thousand kilometers across Europe for charity. I was with a small team, which included my son Sam and nephew Noah, when we found ourselves trapped on the side of the mountain as a huge rockfall caused boulders the size of small cars to fall on us. Throughout all of our challenges, I have never come so terrifyingly close to losing myself, my son, and other teammates, and it all happened in a matter of seconds. We didn't let the experience put us off, and we conquered the summit the next day. The whole team was so unbelievably proud and elated.

DH: When you were a kid growing up, where did you want to visit above anywhere else?
RB: Ever since I watched the moon landings as a child I have looked up to the skies with wonder and dreamt of becoming an astronaut. The Apollo 11 mission was one of my biggest inspirations to set up Virgin Galactic. I couldn't be more proud that Virgin Galactic has completed two spaceflights to date, and I couldn't be more excited to go to space.

CHAPTER 1

FINDING YOUR SEA LEGS

Comfort Is the Enemy of Progress

At the end of my senior year at Western Kentucky University, I started realizing that my plan to be a print journalist for the next thirty years might have some fatal flaws.

I was pretty disappointed because I had very specifically chosen photojournalism over everything. It was the only thing that I knew I was good at. God knows I'd had limited success with math, science, chemistry, geography, spelling—you name it. Photography made sense to me because it was visual.

I think the most exciting aspect of being a photojournalist was all the people that I got to meet. Journalists are always out on new assignments, finding new stories. Sometimes those situations are exciting and fun, and sometimes they're awkward or even difficult, because you're photographing someone at a particularly trying time, or in the wake of tragedy.

Photojournalists get pretty used to meeting people from all walks of life. For me, photographing celebrities, politicians, sports figures, and natural disasters was a great crash course in small talk. You learn how quickly you can get comfortable with almost anyone.

After I graduated, degree in hand, I decided to stay in Bowling Green, Kentucky, to figure out what it was I was going to do for a living.

For my first job post-college, I went to work for a small advertising agency in town, but pretty quickly realized that I wouldn't be finding my future there, either. Not only was the place melting down around me, but I didn't understand why I needed to work for a third party as a photographer when I could just be working for the clients directly.

After one particularly frustrating work trip, I wrote a really long email to my boss at the time pleading with him to change things. Maybe I shouldn't be using my own laptop at work for their client projects? Perhaps I shouldn't be using all my own camera equipment and then getting billed out at $400 an hour, yet only getting paid a hair over minimum wage?

These aren't the kinds of things you would normally bring up to your boss, but I didn't really have a lot to lose, because they appeared to be spinning out of control at the time. In fact, they were purposely only working me thirty-four-and-a-half hours a week to avoid having to pay for my health insurance, even though insurance was largely the reason I had taken the job in the first place.

Unsurprisingly, my email didn't go over too well, so I walked in the next day and handed in my resignation.

One of the people I talked to before I left the building was the graphic designer and art director of the agency, who reassured me that yes, I was making the right decision, that I absolutely should be leaving because the place was crumbling, and not to feel bad.

Unfortunately, my boss clearly disagreed, because he made me call all of the clients I had worked for and talk to them about why I was leaving. These were some of the most awkward phone calls of my life, but ultimately his plan backfired when almost all of the clients immediately asked me if I would continue to do their photography work going forward. I had resigned without a plan, but it now seemed like I had one.

I asked the art director if he could help me create a logo, because I was going to start my own business. I didn't have much money to pay him, but I knew he was talented. I think we agreed on $300.

While he was working on that, I walked across the street, into the county clerk's office, and wrote a check for $11 to a woman named Dot, to start a business.

She asked me what kind of business I wanted to start. I wasn't sure, so she gave me a few options. I decided that the cheapest and easiest would be a sole proprietorship, so I filled out the paperwork for that. When she asked me what I wanted to name my business, I gave her the only name I could come up with: Houghton Multimedia.

I rode my bike home that afternoon pretty proud of myself. I was now an entrepreneur.

My new clients weren't particularly exciting, but I cherished them because they were all I had. Over the next couple of months, to make money, I photographed the insides of banks, head shots for aspiring professionals, and even a few baby pictures for people I knew in town.

I started taking random meetings with anyone I could get a hold of.

I didn't own a home at the time, but like a lot of people, I had rent to pay, so I wasn't picky about the jobs I accepted. I had built a fantastic website, and the offers kept kind of rolling in.

One of the projects I worked on was an overview video for a small local furniture company. They were proud of the fact that everything they sold was made in the USA—in Bowling Green, in fact—but they had very few marketing materials to really explain that to people.

A terrific friend of mine from school named Dallas was working there at the time. He hired me to produce a four- to five-minute video, I think we agreed on $2,000. I had quoted a much higher number, but unfortunately that was the budget. In exchange, I picked up a free outdoor patio set from the showroom floor.

Dallas and I set out to shoot the video, my first major paid project. I got all the equipment I could get my hands on, and away we went.

The day of the shoot, I was standing in one of the warehouses, filming the assembly line.

My phone rang, and a guy named David introduced himself to me and told me that he had seen my website and was a big fan of my work. He wondered if I had the time to come in and meet him and talk about a potential project.

We set the meeting for the following Thursday, and I didn't really think another thing about it.

When the day arrived, I drove to the address, which confused me a little bit because it was a house (a very nice house), and I'd been expecting an office.

David came out to meet me, and invited me inside. I spent the next couple of hours talking with him and another guy named Buddy.

They didn't go into a lot of detail about what they wanted me to do; they really just wanted to look at and talk about the work that I had on my website at the time.

They had a lot of questions about how many people it took to produce the work, and how I had filmed certain things. I showed them as many videos as I could from my Vimeo account. At the time, it had a mix of things I had done professionally, some videos I had done for fun, and a demo reel of my best work set to some music that I had made one night over a case of beer.

One of the pieces I was most proud of was a video called "The Beauty of Digital Film," which you can still find on Vimeo today. It really seemed to capture their attention.

———

A few weeks before, in my newfound unemployment, I was help-ing my grandmother clean out her basement when I happened to run across some old film reels, which looked like they hadn't been used since JFK was in office.

Sitting not too far away in the same closet in that basement was my grandfather's projector, which he had used throughout the forties, fifties, and sixties to watch their home movies.

Intrigued, I put the whole setup together, turned all the lights off, and flicked it on.

I was transfixed by what I saw. Videos from the fifties of my mom and her siblings (she's one of six) playing outside the house they grew up in, where my grandparents had lived for forty-five years. I don't think I had ever seen footage of my mom as a child, and I'd never actually seen an old projector run, either.

I decided immediately to somehow convert this footage to high definition so I could watch it on my computer and edit it. The best way I could think of was decidedly analog: I got my current video camera pointed at the projection screen, did a tight crop on it, turned off all the lights, and got it as in focus as possible. I recorded every second of film I ran across.

I think there were only ten to twelve minutes of footage, but I took my new digital film home and immediately put it together in Final Cut Pro, set to some music. A lot of times I would place music in the background of footage, just to help the editing process. I found this song that I had bought on iTunes, from the soundtrack to some movie, and it fit so perfectly.

It turned out to be one of the best films I ever did. Even though it was my family on-screen, I think anyone could watch it and feel that swell of nostalgia. Clearly, Buddy and David felt it too.

A few hours into the meeting, I realized a couple of things. First, I really enjoyed these people. They were very complimentary about my work, and that was nice, but also they just seemed like people that you'd want to do business with.

Second, I still hadn't figured out anything about what they did for a living, or what on earth they might want me to do for them. Mostly, they asked about my capabilities—what I was able to film and how I edited.

A couple hours later, I walked out through the front door, got into my car, and turned the ignition. Buddy ran after me and signaled for me to roll my window down.

"I need to ask you one more question," he said.

"Okay," I said.

"I need to know how much money you would need to make if you were going to work here full-time."

I didn't really know what he meant by that because I still didn't know what they did. So I looked at him and said, "I don't think there's any way I can answer that question because I have no idea, you know, what you would want me to do."

"Our owner would like to meet you sometime next week. If you can come back. We can tell you a little more about it, but I really do need to understand your salary requirements to see if this is going to be possible," he said.

I just sat there thinking I was on *Candid Camera* or something. How much money do you need to make for a job that you don't know what it is?

I did some quick math in my head and realized that between my salaries from the university, where I was a faculty advisor for the student newspaper, and what I had projected to do with my business that year, I could conceivably clear $80,000.

Now, I have no idea if I actually would have made $40,000 for my business my first year out of the gate. In all honesty, after expenses, probably not.

I looked at Buddy and said, "This is really hard for me to answer, and this isn't a final answer," wanting to make sure I left some negotiating room in case I vastly overshot the runway.

"The best thing I can tell you is I think I would need to make eighty thousand dollars to walk away from my other commitments."

He smiled, said, "Excellent," and started to walk away.

I looked at him and said, "Buddy, I have no idea what it is that you all do, so I'm not sure . . . what you need me to prepare for next week."

He smiled and replied, "I worked at the university for thirty years. That's where you work, right?"

"Yes."

"Trust me, this will be better. I wish I could tell you more, but just stay by the phone, and when we give you a ring about the meeting next week, come by. I think you'll enjoy it."

And then he left.

I drove home a little bit confused. To be honest, I don't think I took the offer very seriously. Nice people and all, but I had no idea why anyone would want to hire you for a role you didn't know anything about, just a few short hours after meeting you.

But sure enough, four or five days later, the phone rang. It was David, asking if I could come by the following day around 1 p.m.

The next day, I dressed a little nicer. For the first meeting, I was in jeans and a T-shirt. I figured if I was going through some sort of job interview I should look a little more professional. I walked into the lobby, and a man that I hadn't met before, named Bill, came over and shook my hand.

He said hello and told me that he would like to introduce me to Mr. Kelley, who was the owner. I sat in the lobby wondering who this owner was. A few minutes later, Mr. Kelley walked down the stairs and came over and shook my hand. "Why don't we go upstairs and chat for a while," he said.

We sat down in a big room with these beautiful leather chairs. Mr. Kelley told me that he had seen the work that I had shown David and Buddy the week before, and that he had really enjoyed it and thanked me for making the time to meet.

I told him a little bit about myself and what I did for a living, where I went to school, and what I was trying to do with my business. He launched into an in-depth conversation about the media industry. Primarily, the discussion centered around how TV channels and industry gatekeepers had gotten lazy and were cranking out crap content that no one wanted to watch.

We joked about twenty seasons of *Survivor* and endless re-runs on TV of the Kardashians. In 2011, on-demand streaming platforms existed but were in their infancy and mostly filled with lower grade shows. We discussed the pending shift in the media landscape that would take place when streaming went mainstream, and how the media companies would be caught flat-footed in a world where consumers got to choose what they wanted to watch whenever they pleased.

I couldn't help but completely agree with everything he said. I talked to him about spending four years in college learning pho-tojournalism only to graduate and look for a job in an industry with no business model. Making great content sounded like a fascinating upgrade from making furniture company videos.

He told me he had been waiting to jump into the media business for years, watching and waiting for the right time. "The Convergence" was a term that had been thrown around for dec-ades to describe the next phase of media evolution, but in reality, it had been slow and painful to materialize.

In my ignorance, I asked him why a guy would want to start a business in an industry that was so upside down.

He told me that the best time to jump into an industry was when it was in flux and people were trying to figure it out. That way, you had a chance to actually shape the landscape. Made sense to me.

At the end of our meeting, he said, "They told me what you need to make, and I'd like you to come work for me. Basically, you'd be doing what you've been doing, but you won't have to worry about going out and trying to find business. I think we can have a lot of success if you'd be willing to come on board. They told me you need to make eighty thousand. How does eighty-five sound?"

I didn't think twice before saying yes. Thinking back on it now, I guess it's not as big a leap of faith as it looked like—after all, what was I leaving behind? I was twenty-one years old at the time, and six months into my new life as a media business owner, part one.

After I accepted, I shook Mr. Kelley's hand and walked out the door wondering what I had just signed up for. Mostly I was excited that I was going to have a job creating content, which is all I'd really ever wanted.

I started a couple of weeks later, and spent the next nine months doing anything and everything I could for Mr. Kelley and all of the projects he had going.

Buddy and David and I became great friends, and I found plenty of opportunities to be useful. Anything that required photography, design, computers, etc., I was on it.

Mr. Kelley and I spent the next year or so developing the concept for a media company with the goal of creating great content. I didn't see him every day, and we didn't live in the same state. But he called at least once a day or every other day with a new set of assignments.

Inevitably, I wound up involved in all sorts of things far outside of the media industry and content creation. I guess the easiest way to describe it is that I more or less functioned as his personal assistant for the first eighteen months.

A year into my new job, I moved down to Nashville, Tennessee, settling just outside of town in a suburb called Franklin. By this time, our company had a total of two employees: me and a designer we had hired, Adam Moore. Adam and his wife agreed to move down to Nashville from Colorado, and turned up to our new office ready to work.

Adam and I spent the first few months staffing up, hiring a video editor and a few assistant editors as well as redesigning the office. Mr. Kelley had a keen sense of interior design and had some particular ideas of how our new office should look.

Soon after, we made a trip to New York City to meet a man named Michael Rosenblum. Michael was well known for producing one of the first reality TV shows, *Trauma: Life in the ER*. He had also helped found news networks like New York 1 and NYT Television, and was a consultant for the BBC.

Michael told us that every news organization in the world was approaching content-gathering at exactly the wrong angle. Why would you need so many people, crews, and big heavy cameras when your content will only have a shelf life of twenty-four hours? Instead, he wanted to train as many people as possible to shoot and edit video on their own. In this mission, he was almost evangelical.

Michael signed on as a consultant for us, and I really looked up to him. Not only did he have an impressive résumé, but he was also a very entertaining guy. He, Mr. Kelley, and I got along really well as we worked through how to get our new media operation off the ground.

In the course of my first year, I had made countless lists with Mr. Kelley of companies that we liked, companies we might acquire, and potential buyers for our burgeoning video content. We broke them down into different categories, including food, adventure, wildlife, and travel.

Travel was such a great category for a number of reasons. Primarily, we liked that it was reasonably agnostic and nonpolitical. Who doesn't want to travel? More than that, the existing type of travel content in 2011 was abysmal. We joked that the Travel Channel was filled with TV shows about ghost stories and tattoo artists. Long gone were the days of Samantha Brown showing people around the world from their living rooms.

I couldn't tell you exactly when or how Lonely Planet wound up on one of our lists, or if that had anything to do with what happened next. I know I had included Lonely Planet in some paperwork I sent to Mr. Kelley, because I still have the screen shots I took on my iPad of Lonely Planet articles, thinking how each of the stories should be an episode of a TV show.

At some point, unbeknownst to me, Michael made a phone call to the BBC (where his wife, Lisa, had worked for many years) and got us a meeting. I was thrilled. Michael, Lisa, and I went to London and sat down with the executives, quickly asking about Lonely Planet. The BBC had bought Lonely Planet a few years earlier, and had a few false starts as they tried to turn it into their in-house travel brand. The global financial crisis happening at the time wasn't helping.

All I was hoping for was the chance to create some TV shows for Lonely Planet. So I didn't know what to think when Mr. Kelley told me he thought we might be able to buy the company.

That would mean that after a year of working on various projects outside of media and content, I was finally going to get my chance to *create* content. Exactly why I had signed on in the first place.

Over the next twelve months, we had various meetings with the BBC talking through the potential deal. At one point, they decided to visit us in Nashville to see our media operation.

A common theme of working with Mr. Kelley was speed. It would be inaccurate to say that things were deadline-driven, because nothing was ever that black and white. The BBC example is a perfect distillation of how we operated.

With the pending meeting just three weeks away, Mr. Kelley sat down with me and outlined an office redesign. It included repainting all the walls of our twelve-thousand-square-foot headquarters, then with an employee head count of four or five. There were several rooms where he wanted to replace carpet with hardwood, and a whole host of furniture requirements to get ready for our meeting a few weeks later.

He was leaving town until just before the meeting, and I told him I would get it done. As it turned out, I wasn't quite sure what I had promised.

Of all the housing market troubles the United States had faced during the economic crisis, Franklin, Tennessee, was somewhat exempt. Construction and new development carried on, and finding contractors with no notice turned out to be incredibly difficult.

Just imagine trying to find, in a town to which you had just moved, a commercial painter, a flooring specialist, an electrician, a plumber, a concrete floor refinisher, and a drywall contractor to start and finish a significant redesign and building project in three weeks.

Adam pitched in and made most of the phone calls to potential contractors, and we started putting a list together of people and prices.

It may seem like a silly thing to be worried about, but the leadership of the British Broadcasting Corporation was flying to our little town in Tennessee, visiting our office, the new media company, to finally see who they might be selling Lonely Planet to.

As our contractor list came together, I was on the phone with Mr. Kelley daily getting budget approvals for the various components and doing my best as a construction foreman. The three components of execution are usually: time, quality, and cost. The long-known truth is that you can generally have only two of the three. To do a job, you're not going to find someone who's cheap, fast, and does quality work. If you want it fast and well done, it's going to be expensive.

Cheap, or should I say, budget-friendly was the anchor of our existence. We continually made things happen with a budget that was a tiny fraction of what anyone would expect, so much so that it was actually a point of pride.

With budget-friendly being a requirement, we started trying to find contractors who were agreeable to our deadlines. The biggest challenge was the hardwood floor. Getting an order of hardwood flooring measured, shipped, delivered, installed, and finished in three weeks for three thousand square feet is essentially impossible.

Mr. Kelley told me he had some hardwood flooring in a warehouse in Kentucky that we could use, so Adam and I drove up and loaded it into a box truck, a few boards at a time, and drove it down to Tennessee.

Our painter, who would later become a maintenance employee for us at Lonely Planet, knew a guy that did hardwood flooring, so we hired him on the spot. Without getting into too much detail, hardwood flooring is mostly installed with an air-pressurized nail gun to attach it to the subfloor. Not our guy. He had a manual nailer that you whacked with a hammer to drive the nail into the wood.

Our office was on the second floor of our building, and the business downstairs recorded a radio show, so making any sort of construction noise during the day was out of the question. Adam and I took turns spending the nights in the office supervising our night shift construction crew over the next few weeks. I still hadn't moved to Tennessee, and was sleeping in a condo we had a few blocks away, riding home once a week or so with Adam, back to Kentucky.

One of the nights I was on duty with the construction crew, their hardwood flooring equipment broke, and work came to a halt. I was standing there looking at our main conference room where the flooring was going in. This was supposed to be the location of our BBC meeting, seven days away. It was a mess. How on earth were we ever going to finish in time?

When Lowe's home improvement store opened the next morning, I met our contractor over there and bought him a new hardwood flooring machine with my own money. I don't think he had the funds to get a new one, and I didn't have the time to wait or waste another hour of construction being halted.

Over the next few days, the pace of the work picked up. Out of a mix of fear of missing our deadline and sheer boredom in the middle of the long nights, Adam and I actually learned how to lay flooring, and took our turns with the hammer, laying and installing one board at a time.

We were having trouble finding someone to do drywall work on our walls, and I was on the phone with my dad, who lived in Atlanta, complaining about trying to find good contractors. Before I knew it, Dad was in his truck and driving the five hours to Nashville. He was our new drywall man and spent the next two days repairing and finishing spots around the office.

The night before our meeting with the BBC, Adam and I were still running around like chickens with our heads cut off trying to get everything ready. Mr. Kelley was going to be in the office the next morning, a little before our meeting was supposed to start, and we were both petrified he wouldn't be happy with our progress.

I had moved into my new house in Tennessee the day before as Adam spent the day at Hobby Lobby buying picture frames and printing posters to hang on the walls so it looked something like a place of business.

The morning of the meeting, when I was driving in around 5 a.m., I got a speeding ticket. Things were not starting out well.

Adam once again beat me to the office before the sun came up and was standing in the lobby when I walked through the door. The place looked incredible. I don't know how long he had been there; I think all night, putting the finishing touches on everything.

A few minutes later Mr. Kelley came in and spent a few minutes quietly walking around the office surveying our work. "It looks great," he said.

Relief.

"Well, to be honest, I wasn't sure if we were going to get it all done in time," I said.

"I didn't think there was any chance you would get half of it done," he replied with a smile on his face.

James McBride

Get out your wallets, you're about to drain your bank account. We'll fly to the Indian Ocean to visit Nihi Sumba, the number one hotel in the world, created by James and pal Chris Burch in 2012.

Recently recognized as "One to Watch" by *Bloomberg Businessweek*'s Bloomberg 50 and awarded Independent Hotelier of the World by *Hotels* magazine, James McBride is a global hotelier who has run some of the world's leading hotels during his twenty-five-year professional career. Known for his limitless creativity, clever marketing techniques, and exceptional hotel experiences, James has raised the bar in the hospitality industry, paving the way for inventive ideas and competitive spirit.

Daniel Houghton: Thank you so much for taking the time. I would love for you to just give me an overview of who you are, your life, and how you got started in travel.
James McBride: Of course. I'm James McBride. I was born in Pretoria, South Africa, in 1964. It was a wonderful place to grow up, in spite of everything. I went off to boarding school when I was eleven. I was in the army for two years, then I went to hotel school. I worked at the Royal Hotel—the best hotel in South Africa—in the kitchen. I loved what I did. I worked all the time. I went to America in 1987 for a vacation, traveling backpack-style, and started looking for a job.

I will say I was very privileged. My grandfather was on the game farm in South Africa, so from a very young age I would go to the bush, cook on the open fire, etc. My father's cousin was at UC Davis, South Africa, and he was doing his thesis on a pride of lions. Into this pride, the first two non-albino, pure white lion cubs were born. They were very worried about poachers coming after the white lions, so unfortunately, they ended up in the zoo eventually.

I joined Ritz-Carlton in its infancy—in 1988, when they were only six. I took the brand to Hong Kong, Singapore, and Kuala Lumpur, then came back and opened one up in Washington, DC, in 1999. When I was at Harvard Business School's executive program, they taught the case of the opening of the Ritz-Carlton hotel in Washington, DC.

DH: That's awesome. I just went through that executive program last year and it was unbelievable.
JM: It was a great experience. Twenty years later, that case is still taught all over the world, and I get involved with it quite a bit.

I've always loved bread cooked on a fire, which inspired my restaurant Firehouse. When we first opened in Washington, DC, there were lots of places trying to grow. So it took working every day and going on this crazy journey around the world to reach the present, where you can fulfill your dream.

DH: Tell me what you want people to know about Nihi Sumba.
JM: It was completely unplanned. My dear friend and business partner Chris Burch . . . when he divorced Tori, I met him at the Carlyle Hotel. Chris was the cofounder of their brand, and we had always wanted to do work together. I was president of YTL at that time, which is a large conglomerate in Singapore.

Chris called me and said, "This place is for sale; would you take a look at it?" I had never heard of Sumba, so I went. I went on a Thursday, came back on a Thursday . . . there was only one charter plane from Bali. So I looked at it, and it kind of reminded me of Africa. It was beautiful—much bigger than Bali, more like the size of Jamaica. It's wild. People still carry swords. It's a Christian island. There were no luxury resorts, but they had a great surf wave, so there was a huge clientele for that. At the time I said that it was great, but it wasn't something that I was interested in.

Chris wanted to buy it—his kids loved to surf. So I helped him put the deal together. I was going about once a quarter to Sumba, where we are going to deploy a little bit of money, but not really blow it out. And I think in the middle of 2013, we finally realized, "This place could be unbelievable." So Chris wired thirty-five million dollars and we built an extraordinary place in the appropriate way, and at the same time grew the Sumba Foundation—educating children, providing portable water, eradicating malaria (now 95 percent are malaria-free). All of the costs of the foundation are underwritten by Chris, and everything we raise goes directly to a cause.

Other CEOs thought, "James McBride has gone completely and utterly mad," but as it became more and more successful, then people think you're brilliant. It became the number one hotel in the world two years in a row (2016–2017). Clearly, one of the first hotels that had been number one two years in a row. And honestly, more press in 2017 than any hotel on the planet. (I've never substantiated that, but I think if I did an exercise, it would be pretty hard to beat.)

We were on the cover of *Departures*, so many covers, on TV, and we got on Instagram very early, in 2013. So many influencers that are big now were not influencers back then. But I became friends with Jeremy (Jauncey, CEO of Beautiful Destinations) and everyone, we all grew up together, and they loved what we did. We never let anyone down. I think because Chris and I already operated in a global context—I've been in the hotel business for a long time—everyone gave you a chance. And before you know it, a very short period of time, we were sitting on this incredible place. But it was real, and not skin deep, and I think that sort of edge of wild experience (which is our tagline) is very powerful. It's real. Then, the advent of the spa—everything you could ever want—is like none other. It's everything that every spa in the world tries to be, but in its natural form.

DH: Yes.

JM: It all happened organically and naturally, without a manual or a plan. But I attribute a lot of success to that feeling of soul, and what makes sense. That's what people want today. People don't want ostentation, they want appropriate luxury. I am not a big fan of eco-branding. I think it's nonsense, to be honest.

DH: Agreed!

JM: For people to give you a cheap shower with no pressure, or make you use the same sheets for a week. I think it's about being appropriate and doing what is right for the specific environment. Make sure you are going to conserve the environment. Responsibility doesn't have to be eco-approved. Unfortunately, these buzzwords just become a way for everyone to get on the bandwagon.

DH: Yes.

JM: And so that journey has continued on. I can't believe, almost seven years into it and the business continues to grow. You know, we've got a space in Costa Rica and we are close to getting spaces in Baja and Los Cabos. We've been given a site by the government in Iceland, in the northeast, that's difficult to underwrite because there is a house and villa concept there. But it's easily the wildest experience yet because it's so exotic.

So that's sort of where we are. I think we have to work hard now to keep reinventing ourselves. People love us, but we don't have the extraordinary tale that we had before. We aren't the new kid on the block, and there are many more off-the-beaten-path places opening.

I hate vanilla experiences, and I think even luxury experiences have become very vanilla. I don't like tables for two with people on honeymoon having dinner together because I think you failed if that's your objective. We have an amazing group of clientele that are worldly, fun, educated, yes, most of them are wealthy, some come on a once-in-a-lifetime trip and they like that they can integrate with each other.

DH: It is, absolutely.
JM: And as much as it's progress and evolution, it does make one worry that everything becomes mainstream when the world is completely connected in every single way.

DH: You've spent your life traveling. When you think back on all the places you've been, which one comes to your mind first? Also, how has travel changed you as a person over time?
JM: I grew up playing polo with my dad, and I was invited on a trip to Mongolia. In the days of Genghis Khan, they used to play with people's skulls. So to play polo in this environment was pretty crazy.

There was so much dancing, and the vodka at night, basking in these beds, swimming in the river to get clean ... I mean, it was just amazing. This led me to participate in British Polo Day, which we did on the beach, teaching the native people how to play. It was beautiful. That trip was probably the one that meant the most to me.

Anyway, I love to travel. I'm always on the move, and I think it becomes addictive—going to new places. I don't think anything stimulates us more. Two weeks ago I went to Haiti, with an invitation from the minister of tourism and the president of the group, to try to figure out a way of building something.

Haiti is such a beautiful place. To find someone that would build a twenty-room place where people could learn about the music, see the orphanages, learn about the arts would be great. I took my son to Cairo on the way to South Africa, and I literally hired the best guides with the best ratings from TripAdvisor. This guy picked us up at the airport. I told him exactly what we wanted. We wanted a boat to go on the Nile. I wanted to go to the highest point by the Pyramid of Giza. I wanted breakfast cooked on the fire, I wanted to see the sunrise. Hire the camels. We did it all.

If you go to my Instagram, @jameswmcbride, you'll see all the stories I've saved of going out in the early morning. Nothing glamorous about it, but the moon was full and the sun rose over the pyramids. It was just me and my son; we went to buy eggs and bread from the bakeries at four o'clock in the morning. Most people visiting would never do that.

And I'm not fearful. I fortunately have a natural ability to put together what I think something should be, or how it should feel. And most of the time it works out—doing it in a natural and exotic way. I just don't want it to be vanilla.

L. David Marquet

Let's talk about a very different type of travel. What do you do when you get assigned to take over command of the US Navy's worst-ranked nuclear submarine? Try something different! Captain David Marquet spent twenty-eight years in the United States Navy and took his submarine, the *Santa Fe*, from worst to first, eventually achieving the highest retention and operational standing in the navy.

David has seen the world from some pretty unusual vantage points, and he was kind enough to share a little about his life and travels. He now spends his time speaking on leadership and writing books, most notably *Turn the Ship Around!: A True Story of Turning Followers into Leaders* (Portfolio, 2013).

Daniel Houghton: I imagine you've seen more of the world than almost anyone else I've met. Tell me a little bit about your adventures over the years.

L. David Marquet: So I was in the navy for twenty-eight years. When I was seventeen or eighteen I went to the Mediterranean, to Spain, saw a bullfight. I went to the UK. The next year I went to Korea and Guam and exotic places I had only read about, and seen pictures of. I did well in the navy; I eventually had the opportunity to captain a nuclear submarine.

We were stationed in Hawaii, which was amazing, and what you do is you go on a six-month deployment. We went to Japan, Okinawa, Tokyo, Singapore, Diego Garcia—which is in a super-cool place in the middle of the Indian Ocean that no one can go to unless you have a military connection—Bahrain, all kinds of places. I saw rafts of sea snakes in the Indian Ocean during mating season. It was like an acre wide; the water was boiling. Just crazy stuff I had never seen before.

We would get a little interaction when we went into port, but interacting with the local populace wasn't our prime reason for being there, and we didn't do a lot of it. A lot of it was structured, a lot of it was scripted. A lot of it was controlled.

And then I wrote this book. Now I, again, travel all around the world. I'm a top-tier United flier, Global Services kind of guy. And the experience is different. It's eye-opening, and reassuring, both.

So for example, I go to some hotel in the middle of Kansas in some town that is important to the people there. But most of the people wouldn't pay much attention to it and I can't remember the name now.

DH: Your average person would have no reason to find themselves there.
LDM: Yeah. And so I'm there in like a Holiday Inn and Conference Center, and it says that and I'm like chuckling to myself, right? But it really was. And so I'm giving this leadership talk to some company. And these people are doing like supercool stuff. Really cool stuff to make the world a better place. And across the hall, there's another company that's also having some kind of a conference. And they're also doing cool stuff.

It's probably not going to put Silicon Valley out of business, but over and over and over wherever I go. I have this, I get on the phone, I call my wife and tell her that I could be in New York.

I had another amazing experience; my book came out in Chinese. And I go to China, which is just crazy to begin with. Right? So here I am a former nuclear submarine commander in Communist China.

I noticed that I kept seeing these two big guys, and they're, like, standing in the back the whole time, ha ha. So I had this event at lunch with a bunch of expats. People running businesses, and they all happened to be expats.

So these are basically Americans and Brits, and Europeans. And they're running the manufacturing arm or whatever of their business. And my book on leadership is about giving people control, letting them make decisions, because you'll have a more resilient, more robust company, and they'll actually like their jobs. But it takes the leader courage to say, "Yeah, that's your call, you guys, let me know what you got, what you're gonna do with that."

And then they kind of like give me the sort of, you know, pat on the head. And they say, yeah, this is all great. And we love this. And if we were in the Netherlands, this will really work . . . Chinese people just don't like that. They like to be told what to do and blah, blah, blah.

So I didn't argue with them. I just kind of tucked that away for later. So that night, which turned out to be one of the most amazing experiences of my life, I went to a local university, which they are telling me is like the Harvard of China.

So I walk in this auditorium. It's an executive MBA program. I look around at six hundred faces. All Chinese, and me, one Western dude, and I have a translator. This eighty-five-pound Chinese university student, but she was super-awesome. By this time it was like the fourth event that we had done together, and she *was* me. *She* was the submarine commander, that's how good she was at translating.

So I look over at her, and look at the crowd, and look at her, and look at the crowd. And for some reason, I think I was jet-lagged or whatever, and I just had this "fuck it" moment in my head. So I said, "Hey, guys, here's what I've been told. I was just at this other event and they told me, number one, Chinese people just like to be told what to do." And I kind of said it with a little bit of a, like spitting the words. And I said number two, "If I give you guys a chance to ask questions, none of you will." And then I said, "So take two minutes. Talk to the person next to you about that. And then I want to see what you guys think." And I said, "Ready?" And she sees them over there ready to go.

And as soon as I said it, before she even translated it, the whole place erupted in noise. And then for the next hour and a half, going past my scheduled talk time, all I heard, over and over and over again, was, you know, "That's BS. That's just what you guys think about us. Of course, we want jobs that matter. Of course, we want meaning in our lives. Of course, we want our kids to have a better life than we had." And I was blown away. I never touched my clicker and never used my slides.

I got out of there, and I call my wife, and I said, "I could be in Kansas." You know, what they want is what we want. And now I use that story because over and over and over again I get people telling me they always have a reason why they can't actually trust their people. And I just think it's all BS and they're just making excuses, because basically, we're all the same.

What humans want, no matter where you are, is the same. We might be starting in different places. India was tough. I had a client in Bangalore and spent a week there. You know, and it was probably thirty different places. But once you get people honest, and talking about their dreams and passions, you're like, oh, you're just like me, dude.

So that's my . . . that's the optimism. Because I'm an engineer, and I'm a nuclear guy. And I tend to look at what, how could this get fucked up? And how could this go wrong? And I think this sort of, this natural, I think that part of me is naturally a part of the environment that I came up in, but it's mitigated by this optimism. That every time I come back from my trip, and I see amazing people doing amazing things all over the world, it gets me. I can actually watch the news and not want to kill myself.

DH: Yeah, I'm definitely an optimist. But running a business, you know, made me . . . well, you have to be prepared for things to go wrong. You just have to have a smile on your face when other people are scared shitless.
LDM: Exactly.

DH: What inspired you to go to the Naval Academy, as a young person trying to figure out what your life was going to be?
LDM: We were in the middle of the Cold War. I started high school in 1973 and graduated in 1977. And we went through the oil shocks, and Vietnam was winding down. I was kind of a history geek. I was an introvert; I traveled by reading books. And I believed in the model of society represented by the Constitution of the United States, that the government protects your freedoms. And you can choose your religion, your spouse, your profession, you'll be safe in your home, that kind of thing. It just seemed like a better way.

So I wanted to do my part. And if you're a geek and an introvert, and you go home one day, and you tell your parents you're going to join the military, the only way you get away with it is if you say, "Oh yeah, and I read about these things called submarines, and your job is to hide from people."

DH: A couple of kids from my high school wound up on submarines. And they were the introverted, but super-intelligent

ones, like really smart. But you would never know it because most of the time they didn't turn in their homework. You thought they were poor students, they barely spoke in school, and then you find out they are a nuclear engineer.

LDM: Exactly, yeah, that was me. That was me in high school. That was exactly me.

So the way it works is, you join a tribe, submarines or surfer ships or pilots or Marine Corps. And then that's basically the tribe that you're in, though you may do an exchange program or visiting tour, and you do staff time.

So you'd be at sea on a submarine, and then you would come in and you'd be stationed at the Pentagon or at a headquarters staff or research facility for a couple years, then you go back out to sea.

DH: So you were preparing to take over one submarine, and suddenly, you're in charge of a completely different one, with not-so-great results.

LDM: I came out of the model of leadership called a knowing-telling model, wherein the job of the leader is to know the answer so that they can tell the team what to do. And it's telling the team what to do that results in us getting stuff done. And then we get rewarded for getting stuff done. Luckily, I was really good at that—telling people what to do.

So I keep getting promoted, I'm going to be a submarine captain, and then they say, "Yeah, no, we got another submarine, the *Santa Fe*, worst submarine in the fleet, worst morale, and by the way, the captain just quit a year early, because things are so bad."

So instead of going to the ship I was prepared for, I go to this other ship. The physics of the submarine were the same, but all the buttons and all the equipment were different on each ship. So I walk on board, and it was like—you know the moment in *Star Wars* when they go into the bar?

DH: My favorite scene!

LDM: Yeah, right. You're like, what? Well, that was basically the way it was for me. I'm bewildered, I'm asking questions that I don't know the answers to. So I immediately started telling people what to do, because of course, that's what they expect. And that's what I was programmed for.

I gave an order which couldn't be done on the ship. But the officers tried to make it happen anyway. Nothing really bad happened, but it was kind of embarrassing. I got the guys together. And I say, "I think we are in deep trouble here. Because I spent the last twelve months learning a different ship, different buttons, different pipes, different valves, and you guys are trained to do what you're told."

DH: And they are going to do whatever you tell them.

LDM: Exactly. So if it's good, we live. If it's bad, we die. And they're just looking at their feet, kind of nodding. Then one guy mutters, "Yeah, we figured that out two weeks ago when you showed up."

So I told them, I need you to take initiative. I need you to be you, and you're all empowered, and I want you to speak up if what I say is wrong.

Instead of managing downward, we're all going to look upward. And in the end, I just said hey, tell me what you intend to do. "I intend to submerge the submarine, load a torpedo. Change the menu for lunch." If I don't say no, the answer is yes. But you have to tell me why it's the right thing to do. And I get to ask questions.

But as long as I don't say no, the answer is yes. And that shifted the whole gang. And, like, the rest is history—we won awards, we had the highest morale, we set records for retaining people, and how well we operated the submarine. But it took ten years to play out. The really cool thing is that ten of my officers have since been selected to be submarine commanders, which is a really high number, really hard to do.

DH: So it's like you're in the NFL, and your coaching tree turned out to be insanely successful.
LDM: Exactly.

DH: I've never gotten to ask anyone what it is like to travel on a submarine. To be underwater with this group of men and women for what I can only imagine must be some long periods of time.
LDM: Oh, it's a very intimate experience. You have a hundred and forty people, but we only have a hundred and seventeen beds. So some people are sharing. First of all, it's a lot slower than going on a jetliner, so you really don't get jet lag. You do reset the clock, but we can pick what time we want it to be, because no one sees the sun, right? So normally we follow the local time, just because it allows us to do operational planning; it just seems more logical.

But it's generally a smooth ride. I mean, when the storm comes, we just go deeper. You're looking at the charts, you get to hear all the sounds of the ocean, you get to hear the whales, shrimp, fish, oil wells, distant ships—and that's kind of cool.

DH: Talk to me about transitioning back to civilian life, traveling with a different purpose.
LDM: Well, just in general, it took a while for my brain to adjust

to not needing permission from anybody to do anything. That sounds obvious, but it was a process.

When I got out, my son was an exchange student in Majorca, of all places. Really suffering as a college student, ha ha. And we're kind of both history geeks. So I said, "Wouldn't it be cool if we could visit the Napoleonic battlefield? We'll get a car and drive around at the end of your semester." And I kept talking about it, and finally, he's like, "Dad, why are you saying, 'Wouldn't it be cool?' Why don't you just buy the ticket?"

So we did that, and it was supercool. But for some reason, in my head, I wasn't giving myself permission. Finally, I got over that. And then the next thing I screwed up is I started doing all these talks. I would fly in somewhere the night before, get up, do my talk, go back to the airport, fly out to the next place.

And sometimes I did two talks in two different countries in one day. It was an awesome opportunity, but a crazy schedule. So now everywhere I go, I try and have a plus one.

And I'm always asking my team, what's my plus one? It could be visiting a museum, it could be going on a trail run. I like exploring the trails. It could be reconnecting with an old friend that I haven't seen—anything not work-related. And that has enriched my experience.

DH: What is your favorite plus one that you've done over the years? I love that concept. And I try to do the same thing on each trip.

LDM: Well, my daughter is in London. So probably being able to see my kids. But I really like these trail runs. Like I said, I'm an introvert. I put on my shoes, I look at my map. I ask the locals and I set out on these trails, it's probably not the smartest thing to do.

But I head off on these trails by myself, go out for three or four hours with water. Not knowing what's around the next corner.

If you don't pay attention, every single step, you step on a rock, you're going down. And it's that need to focus in an ever-changing environment. You can't be thinking about work. You're just out there, and then you meet people on the trail. Everybody's a friend, right? It's us against the trail.

DH: What comes to mind when you think about how travel has changed you over the years?
LDM: I grew up in a suburb outside of Boston. It was sort of a big deal when integration was introduced in the school. I can't remember a black kid in our school. And then we had this program where we brought some kids in from the city. But it was kind of a, it was like a, there was an artificial reality and novelty to it; it didn't feel organic.

And so now, when you're on the Shanghai subway, and you're the only white dude, you realize what that must have felt like. And you realize these people just want the same things that we want. And they want better lives for their children just like we do. For me, I think it's helped me become more accepting, and more resistant to this labeling that we tend to do with different groups, whether by their ethnicity or gender preference, or whatever. And I know, when I'm really honest with myself, that I still do this. But I think my ability to listen with curiosity is better.

This is one of the things I really work on, and I always feel like I can be better. But my life is definitely richer and more interesting, because rather than just pushing things away, I open the door a little bit. I say, "Yeah, tell me. Tell me about that."

CHAPTER 2

WHAT'S A P&L?

Taking Every Opportunity

The conversations with the BBC continued on and off for the next year, until we finally had an agreement in place. I had made numerous trips to Melbourne, Australia, where the largest Lonely Planet office was at the time, as well as to London.

The previous CEO of Lonely Planet was moving on, and there was no one scheduled to be running the business once the sale was complete. He announced his departure at the same meeting where we were introduced as the new owners.

One day in our office in Tennessee, Mr. Kelley and I sat down, and the conversation turned to Lonely Planet leadership. I asked him who was going to run the business, and he looked confused. "We are going to run it, what are you asking?" he said.

"Well . . . the CEO is leaving, people are going to be wondering who's in charge. They will know we are the new owners, but *who* in the business is going to be in charge?"

"We are," he replied.

"Yeah . . . I know we are, but—"

He interrupted me. "You are. You and I are going to do it together."

I wasn't asking him because it was a job I wanted. You may have a hard time believing it, but that wasn't even on my radar. The thought hadn't even crossed my mind. I was still in so much shock that we were actually going to own Lonely Planet, the business I had grown up traveling with, a real, incredible, and loved media company.

He stressed to me that it was not a big deal, and that I shouldn't overthink it. We were in this together. With that, we moved on to our next topic.

When the sale announcement was finally scheduled, I flew down to Australia to make a joint statement with the BBC.

BBC executive Marcus Arthur was in charge of Lonely Planet at the time, and was going to be making most of the remarks during the staff meeting before introducing me.

Marcus is from Scotland, and he's the picture of Scottish perfection. He has a smile that can capture a room and the confidence and presence when speaking to an audience that would make anyone pay attention and listen.

He sat me down a few minutes before the announcement and asked me if I had spent much time doing any kind of public speaking. I'm sure he could tell I was nervous. He probably also realized it would be a little awkward for a twenty-three-year-old American kid to stand in front of a global team of seasoned employees at LP and tell them I was going to be their leader.

He looked me right in the eye and said, "Take some deep breaths and be yourself. That's all you have to do. Tell them what you're excited about and how much respect you have for the brand. I'll be up there with you the whole time."

It was the kind of pep talk a coach would give the quarterback right before a big play, and it filled me with the confidence I needed to get it down.

The meeting location was right in the middle of the multistory office that LP occupied—on the second-floor staircase, in fact, so people could gather around from all floors and watch.

I was super-nervous, especially since one of the things I had to cover was that our financial picture as a business was not very healthy. We were going to need to make some changes.

After Marcus said his part, I introduced myself and told the staff who I was, and what we were going to try to do. I can't imagine what they thought. I was only twenty-three years old and had never run a business before.

Afterward, Marcus walked me around the office to meet various groups of the employees and answer questions. Answering questions was the last thing I wanted to do immediately after surviving my first public speaking engagement. I fielded a diverse assortment of inquiries that were much more direct than I was expecting.

I was asked about my age, what the hell I knew about running a business, and exactly what our plans were. It became clear that there was a lot of confusion around why anything needed to change. This surprised me, because the staff was well aware that the numbers weren't great. Somebody actually looked at me and exclaimed, "I just don't understand why we have to make money. I thought this was about travel."

After surviving the Australian meetings, I got on an overnight flight to London, with a stopover in Singapore. Luckily, I was in a business-class seat and could get some sleep, as I hadn't slept well in days. When I got off the plane in London, I took the Tube to the BBC office where the Lonely Planet London team of around one hundred people worked. I walked through the front door, still dazed and confused, and was greeted by an LP employee named Tom Hall.

The first thing he said to me was that we had an all-staff meeting in twenty minutes. The last thing I wanted to do was to repeat the previous day's awkward all-staff announcement, but it was too late. The London office leader had already scheduled the meeting.

He looked at me and apologized and said, "I know this isn't what you wanted to do, but why don't I go up onstage with you? I'll ask you a couple of questions, and I'll make sure we don't get too deep on anything."

"That would be great, but we are just going to cancel it, and you and I can walk around and informally talk with all of the teams."

"Well, they are already seated, waiting for you to join," he replied.

Tom put a microphone on me; he walked onstage and kicked off the meeting before introducing me. I went onstage to say hello to everyone. I think I was only a few words into the sentence "Hi, my name is Daniel," when the entire audience erupted in laughter.

What had happened? Did I forget to wear pants? Was my hair sticking up? Did I have something in my teeth? It was apparent I must have just done something incredibly stupid to have everyone laughing uncontrollably.

I noticed someone at the back start pointing, and I turned around onstage and realized there was a movie theater–size projection behind me. It took me a couple of seconds to realize what I was looking at, but after I gathered my thoughts, it was pretty obvious. It was a gigantic depiction of the scene where Daniel from the Bible is thrown into the lion's den, and everyone is expecting that he's going to die.

I wasn't quite sure who at the time, but someone had made a pretty lousy joke at my expense. I think I started laughing because I didn't know what else to do and it seemed better than bursting into tears for being made fun of in front of the team.

I took a few steps back and jogged off the stage, pulling my phone out of my pocket. I think most people were pretty confused as to what I was doing.

I said out loud, "That's fantastic. I love that painting. If you guys don't mind, I'm actually just going to take a photo of this because I really want to remember this a few years from now."

I figured that was as good an icebreaker as anything and made people realize that I could roll with the punches.

After I took my picture, the painting disappeared pretty quickly, and Tom and I went back onstage, and the meeting got underway. I can barely recall anything we discussed. The truth was, they were right. I really didn't know what I was doing.

Running a global business that has already been around for forty years is no easy task. I knew that I loved the company, and that it was filled with talented people. I was hoping some of them would decide to take me in after all.

And they did. My first, welcome mentor at LP was the chief financial officer, Theo.

A few weeks earlier I had sat in front of the entire Lonely Planet executive team, including Theo, at the KPMG offices in Melbourne, Australia. He had looked at me and asked if I would like to review the P&L.

"That sounds great," I said. "What's that?"

My response didn't land too well. Most of the room looked a little shocked.

"The profit and loss statement," Theo replied. He politely explained that it was the financial record for the performance of the business. The P&L was crucial for understanding what revenues were coming in and what costs were going out.

After that meeting, Theo pulled me aside and said to me, "Why don't you and I have some time one-on-one to review this and I'll walk you through everything?" He spent the next several weeks meticulously explaining primary global accounting to me. Not only how to read the P&L, but the fundamentals of the business, what the key drivers were. He was careful not to try to influence my opinion; the purpose of our time together was just for me to learn.

He indulged as many stupid questions as I could come up with as I tried to get my head around what it even meant to run such a large business.

It's difficult to explain to you just how incredible it was to have someone not judge me for my lack of knowledge and just be there to try to help. Over the next several years, Theo was my closest confidant. I'll never forget the time and patience he showed me as I tried to get up to speed.

As I flew around the world over the next several months, I had a lot of time to think. I had bitten off way more than I'd ever bargained for. After all, I was just trying to find a job where

I could keep traveling. Now I found myself running one of the most famous travel companies on earth. Talk about overshooting the runway.

The international travel was . . . brutal. We had essential offices on three different continents, and between my trips to Australia and England, I was flying around trying to recruit a digital team to launch an overhaul of our website, mobile apps, and sales strategy.

In one two-week stretch in my first year, I flew around the world three different times in opposite directions. Most of the time I didn't know where I was, what time zone I was in, or where I was supposed to be going next.

A lot of places I went to were just for a day or two. There was an entire tour through our European partnerships' headquarters, and many trips to our London office. In my first twelve months alone, I went to London fourteen times.

Over the next five years, the company really started to turn around and come into its own. We had a new digital strategy and platform, and were lucky enough to make *Fast Company*'s World's Most Innovative Companies list, something I'll always be really proud of.

When I walked out the door on my last day, ready for my next adventure, I had logged just over a million miles traveling for Lonely Planet. It was absolutely the hardest thing I've ever done, but it was a privilege to lead such a fantastic team of global travelers.

It certainly wasn't a cakewalk, though. All that time away from home isn't good for relationships, and I wound up divorced from my wife two years into my time at LP. Luckily, I was surrounded by friends and family who have continually supported me. They always made me feel like what I was doing wasn't crazy, and helped me see the light on the dark days.

More than anything, the team I worked with over the years made it all worth doing. To the many, many people who have helped me along the way in any sort of capacity, thank you from the bottom of my heart.

Bruce Poon Tip

Entrepreneur and philanthropist Bruce Poon Tip is the founder of the award-winning adventure travel company and social enterprise G Adventures.

Following a transformational backpacking trip to Asia, Bruce had an idea to change the face of travel. In 1990, at the age of twenty-two and on two maxed-out credit cards, Bruce started G Adventures, a tour operator designed to bridge the divide between backpacking and mainstream travel, and to connect travelers with local people in the countries they visit.

Fast-forward twenty-eight years: G Adventures is now the world's largest small-group adventure travel company, with twenty-eight offices worldwide. They host two hundred thousand travelers per year, offer more than seven hundred tours, and travel to one hundred countries—across all seven continents.

Bruce and I first met in 2014, during the filming of a travel video for Mashable, which you can still find on YouTube. We pretty quickly figured out we thought a lot alike, and we became friends on the spot. We've often found ourselves in the same remote corners of the world at the same time and have always managed to say hello and grab dinner when our schedules align.

Daniel Houghton: Okay, well, I know a lot about you, but the readers do not. So to start, I would love for you to just give me two minutes on who you are, what you do, and what sparked your passion for travel.
Bruce Poon Tip: I'm the founder of G Adventures. I started G Adventures twenty-eight years ago. Almost twenty-nine actually,

in September 1990, when travel was just very different—before the internet, email, and even widespread use of fax machines. And we had the idea of a purpose-driven business model that was connected with local people and cultural immersion.

That's really what the focus was originally. We really got involved in the social enterprise community very early on—there was no real term for it then. And we've gone through a lot of evolutions over our twenty years, from the emergence of ecotourism in the mid-nineties to the idea of responsible travel, which came shortly after that. When sustainable tourism really came into fashion, we were already on our own path.

And now we consider ourselves kind of a model social enterprise. We feel we transcend the travel industry, and engage our customers to a much higher purpose. Specifically, we believe travel can be the greatest form of wealth distribution that the world's ever seen, when people are traveling to the poorest countries in the world.

DH: As soon as you're stepping off the plane, you're spending dollars, right?
BPT: Yes, and if done right, travel can transform people's lives. So I think that the lost opportunity within the industry is we don't embrace that travel can be a force for good. And we're kind of a model for that; we have been for a very long time.

Now, it was a thankless job back in 1995, before the term microfinance even existed, when we started doing community projects, and investing in individuals and small businesses to run our operations.

DH: I'm going to encourage readers to read your book, because you go into a lot of depth on why that model made so

much sense to you, and how you have remained friends with and done business with so many of those same people for decades now.

Readers: Bruce's book is called *Looptail: How One Company Changed the World by Reinventing Business.*

Talk to me about how you have ingrained that into the culture at G Adventures.

BPT: Yeah. I mean, it's, that's a hard question to answer because it's at the core of our existence, our culture and our values as a business. We, like every other company, are aggressive, growth-focused, entrepreneurial, innovative. But at the same time, the social impact side of our business is intrinsically involved in our DNA.

And we do a lot of things to curate our company culture, to make sure we attract and retain the best talent in the world. And stay really focused on customer experience.

DH: And the nice perk is, it's actually a great thing for growth, right? It gets people out there on the road.

BPT: Yeah, that's what the whole looptail theory is about. We believe that travel is the fastest path to peace. If people just got to get out more and learn about other cultures, it would give them a greater sense of their place in the universe and a greater appreciation of where they come from.

DH: Absolutely. Bruce, talk to me a little bit about that nature of your business. You guide people around the world—a great service, since it can be very intimidating to a lot of people when they don't speak the language, or they're not sure

about the culture, or they've seen something bad about that country on the news.

Talk to me about some of the benefits of being able to explore a place with someone that's local, that's been there before, that is proud to show you their home country.

BPT: Yeah, I mean when you get people that are like-minded together who want more from their holiday time, it brings a magical kind of feeling to the group. Because we are global, people from one hundred and sixty different countries book trips with us. When you get on a tour, first of all, you're grouped with people from all over the world. And then you're experiencing another culture together.

That learning, and that kind of community that's created, is invaluable. We offer so much more than most tour companies in terms of community and positive local impact, but we're also about creating a really special experience of discovery just within your group. You're kind of forming a new civilization together. Does that make sense?

DH: Absolutely. Because in some of the far-flung places that you take people, it can be kind of daunting to go it alone. And it's really nice to know that you're going to have a good experience there. I think it's a wonderful way to remove a barrier for people, for instance, if you wanted to go back on your own someday or take your family.

BPT: Oh yeah. I mean we vet everything and we curate everything to give people a unique experience, so we know how daunting it can be! Everyone's motivation to travel is different. We certainly offer the security of a group, but also the freedom of independent travel, because we can be flexible—our groups are small. For people who want to travel and don't have a friend that necessarily wants to go with them, we have a group of friends that will.

When we can bring together a like-minded group of people who book for the right reason, it's magical. So it's our goal kind of to get the best people and the right people on our trips. That's why we are so forward on our purpose-driven model, because it attracts a certain type of person. Originally, people said we shouldn't emphasize it so much, because you're going to eliminate a lot of people, but we believe we should draw that line in the sand. These are our values, this is our purpose, and even though it's polarized our audience, it also created that magic.

DH: Absolutely. Okay, a little bit of a personal question. Talk to me about a place in the world—maybe you've been there or not, it doesn't matter—that you want to take your family to see. You want to make sure that you get to witness your children experiencing it for the first time.

BPT: Okay, I wish you'd asked me this two weeks ago.

DH: Did you just do it?

BPT: We just did, we went to India, and then a year before that was the other one, was Galápagos. I was dying to take them there, because those are two places I've been to, you know, a hundred times. But seeing it again, through their eyes, and giving it that new energy, was so beautiful for me.

Another big one for me is coming up this summer—Japan. I've been there so many times. I almost get jaded, it's so familiar. But I can't wait to see it through their eyes.

Charlie Clifford

If you've ever stepped into an airport, nearly anywhere on the planet, you've seen a TUMI bag. Charlie founded TUMI in 1974, and although he has since sold the business, he's still crafting and selling the best luggage on the market.

Daniel Houghton: Charlie, thanks for taking the time to do this. To start, I'd love to get a quick overview of who you are and what you've done. How did you wind up in the industry?
Charlie Clifford: I grew up in a small town in New Jersey—only about five thousand people. My family didn't do a lot of traveling. We vacationed in Vermont from time to time, where my father's family was from; his grandparents had emigrated from Ireland. All of his family had come down from Vermont and ended up in the New York, New Jersey area, I guess probably sometime in the thirties and forties. So we used to travel to a lake near Rutland, Vermont.

That was kind of the extent of my travel. My father worked for the New York Central Railroad. He was a freight analyst. My parents weren't very adventurous, and we didn't have a lot of money. I wanted to see a different part of the country, so I went to the Midwest for college, and that was my first experience with a metropolitan area.

I ended up at Indiana University, and I spent five years there—three years of undergraduate and two years of business school. I think the stereotype that people are friendlier in the Midwest actually holds up. I think people are more inclined to reach out to people, more down-to-earth. Whereas in the Northeast, people are terrific once you get to know them, but it's more difficult. It is faster-paced, and people have more complicated lives because of the commuting and so forth. So I had a great experience there.

After business school, instead of going into the typical corporate marketing job, I decided to apply for the Peace Corps, a specific program where they recruited MBAs to go to Peru and work with small businesses. So that was my first opportunity to really travel. I had the benefit of a couple of months of language training at Stanford University, so I went to Peru with at least enough Spanish to order meals and ask if there were any houses to rent.

My wife entered the Peace Corps with me. We met at Indiana, where she was a graduate student. She had earned her master's degree in counseling. This was during the Vietnam War; I had a medical deferment for a condition that almost kept me out of the Peace Corps. But I decided that having an international experience, in addition to the academic training I had, would better prepare me for life. So, we went to Peru in 1967, we were there until 1969. That really shaped my view of the world. My first international experience was in a developing country with a culture that was very, very different from everything I had ever experienced.

DH: And when you got out of the Peace Corps, how did you figure out what you wanted to do?
CC: Well, coming out of the Peace Corps, I moved back to the New York area and took a job with the Grand Union Company, which was primarily a food retailer. In the end, food retail was not for me, but I ended up working for one of their subsidiaries, in

industrial marketing. I got my first real exposure to the business world. After doing that for, I guess, four-plus years, I decided that I wanted to do something more entrepreneurial. Corporate life was interesting, but the process of advancement required working in different departments, and was just a little bit too routine.

So I ended up working with a company from the Midwest, which was run by the former associate director of the Peace Corps. They were importing handcrafts, and it was my responsibility to sell the product line in the Northeast. I invested a few thousand dollars in the business and was a shareholder, so I had a chance to get a bird's-eye view of what running a small business was about.

After less than a year of doing this, it was clear that it would be more advantageous for the company to focus on leather goods. The two owners of the company wanted to continue to work with a number of different South American companies on a range of products, from sweaters and wall hangings, to handwoven rugs, to costume jewelry. So their diversity of product had to be sold to different types of stores, and different departments. It was complicated. I felt that by focusing on leather goods, we could sell products that were all produced to the same specifications, whereas typically with handcrafted products, the size and color of the product might vary from what was ordered. The store owners could never really get a handle on what "handcrafted" meant, so they were often thrown by the difference between the samples and what they ultimately received.

My colleagues did not want to focus on leather goods, so I ended up doing it myself. In the early days, I had a partner who handled the administrative part of the business—finance and operations—and I focused on the front end, sales and customer relations, and product development. And that was back in 1975.

DH: As a luggage expert, talk to me about the advice you give to people when they are first traveling. We all take stuff with us. Do you have a philosophy on that?

CC: Well, I'm sure my wisdom, if you want to call it that, is pretty similar to most of the frequent travelers that you have talked to. In today's age, you want to do two things. You want to buy luggage, in my opinion, that is well made. You want a product that will perform well over time. The last thing a traveler wants is luggage that fails—where components break, wheels break, handles break, zippers break, stitching comes undone—because when you're traveling, the last thing you want to do is take time to look for a replacement piece.

Wheeled luggage has become pervasive in the last twenty-five years. It's just so much easier to move around. Way back when, there was luggage that was sold with four wheels, but it didn't stand upright; it would lie on its side. You'd pull it with a leash, and it was always falling over. It was better than carrying something by hand, but it was rather awkward.

So upright two-wheeled luggage came along in the nineties, and since then has been superseded by four-wheel upright luggage, which you can really wheel effortlessly.

The other form that has become very, very popular is the backpack. There are backpacks specifically designed for travel that can accommodate virtually as much as a carry-on. In fact, some of the larger ones carry more than a carry-on. They are soft-sided, whereas most luggage is semi-soft-sided or hard-sided. And, if you are fit enough, you can put that thirty or forty pounds on your back. Backpacks allow you to travel with your hands free. A backpack is a great way to travel, particularly for people with their mobile devices today, constantly looking at things on apps and texting. Not a top-loading backpack, though. You need to get a backpack that zips around, that opens up like a suitcase so that if you're using it for a travel bag, you can pack it and unpack it easily.

So I would recommend people look at four-wheeled luggage that is high-quality, designed to last for years and years, or a backpack that is made for travel.

DH: I've always tried to live that rule where you lay everything out and then get rid of half of it. And I've never gone wrong with that. In fact, it is a little bit of an obsession of mine to try to make sure that everything I am taking I am actually going to use on this trip.

CC: Well, I think you're absolutely right. My other rule is to put everything you need in a carry-on rather than checking luggage. It just saves time at the airport, both checking in but particularly when you're waiting for your luggage. Sometimes you can wait thirty to forty-five minutes for the luggage to come down in an airport that isn't very efficient at baggage handling.

DH: Yeah, it's crazy. I think I've almost never broken that rule. I even went skiing in Europe last year and carried boots with me and stuffed them in the overhead bins. I'll do just about anything to not check a bag.

CC: Yeah, no question. I think that learning to pack—typically, if you are seeing different people on different days, being able to wear something more than once and to mix and match your outfits so that you're not wearing the same thing every day is important. Of course, if you're traveling for an extended period of time, then getting your clothes washed or cleaned is a way to travel without two thirty-inch suitcases.

DH: Absolutely. I've never been shy about sending some clothes to the hotel laundry. I've never had anything lost, and it will basically allow you to travel anywhere with a carry-on in my opinion.

CC: The only challenge with that is that you have to be at the hotel for more than one night.

DH: Correct. Yeah, sometimes you have to check the express service box with a premium on the price to make sure that you get it by five a.m. And while we are on the topic of luggage, talk to me a little bit about your new luggage line, named ROAM. The products look great.

CC: Well, I think that over the past several decades more and more people have been traveling with black luggage. Black luggage doesn't show the dirt, and so it's always in style. It always looks good. But with that has come sort of a sea of black luggage. We think that in this day and age, people want to express their personality. They do that through the clothes they wear, how they furnish their home, the kind of car they drive, the different products they use. And to a degree, there has been a lot of "sameness" in the world of luggage.

We think the market is ripe for an option where people can actually design their own color combinations and end up with a customized piece of luggage. This isn't possible for other manufacturers because 98 percent of the luggage in the world is made in Asia, in factories that are designed around the premise of mass production, with very large minimum order quantities. Typically there are five hundred to one thousand pieces per color, per style . . . or more if somebody wants to get the best possible price. And the lead times are very long—typically three months to produce, one month to ship. And so we decided that we would produce luggage in America. It's basically made to order. We have a website where people can go, and in ten minutes or so can choose the different color components for their luggage. And they end up with a personalized piece of luggage which reflects their own individuality.

DH: Fantastic. I'm going to make sure we have a link to that in the book so people can find it.

Readers, check out ROAM at www.roamluggage.com.

CC: And to be consistent with my philosophy of luggage, it is top-quality. The material is polycarbonate, which is extremely strong, resilient, and super lightweight, and it's made in America. Some of the other components are sourced overseas because we essentially wanted to get the best possible components, from the best manufacturers. But it's also priced at 30-plus percent below other premium brands, because we're making in America and we're primarily direct-to-consumer. And we've made no compromise in quality.

DH: It can definitely take a beating; you can see that on the website.
CC: We will be happy when we count you as a customer, Daniel.

DH: I was actually just picking out my color combination! So let's talk about some of the places you've been over the years. When you think back on all the different countries and continents, what are the ones that keep coming back to mind?
CC: Well, I think the most profound experience of traveling, of course, was my first international travel to Peru; we also had an

opportunity to travel to some of the other South American countries. Peru is just a fascinating country. I am embarrassed to say it took me over forty years to get back. My wife and I went in 2012. It was just a very heartwarming experience to go back to a country where we had experienced so much goodwill and where our views of the world had broadened. I had the benefit of seeing how the US is viewed by people in the developing world, whose number one priority was improving their lives day to day.

It's a very friendly, very warm culture where people are naturally curious. They like to meet people, and they're proud of their country. There is an infectious enthusiasm for food and for culture. Going back forty-plus years later, it was great to see the changes in the country. The country has certainly modernized in many ways. It's much more populous, with forty million people today, but they still have a very large indigenous population.

The language of the Incas is still spoken by (I think) about 40 percent of the population. Lima is a sophisticated, international city. The mountains of Peru are where you can still feel the connection to the ancient Incan Empire. We had an opportunity to travel up to Cusco, which is just a world-class historical city—it was the Incas' capital city. So Peru is probably at the top of the list.

In terms of singling out other countries, I don't know, I've been to probably about fifty different countries around the world. Almost every single one of them has something positive about them to remember. It's very hard to single them out—Italy, Spain, France, England. Going into cities like Prague and Vienna; the Scandinavian cities, Stockholm, Copenhagen, Helsinki. Amsterdam is a terrific city, with the canals and the Old World feeling.

So I think that gaining the perspective of how other people look upon the international order, and where the US fits into that, is important. When you hear people in other countries talk about their worldview, you suddenly realize that we have to look beyond our borders and do some listening as well as talking.

DH: Absolutely. I grew up in a fairly nonpolitical household, but raised by traveler parents, and I think the biggest thing about travel is that you can't help but pay attention to how other people view Americans, and our influence in the world. It doesn't mean you have to compromise your views or your belief system or anything you hold on to culturally, I just think it gives you a real fresh perspective on why some people might think differently. And it's harder to grasp without spending real time someplace else.

CC: Well, I think that there are different solutions to the challenges that every country, every culture faces today. I think it's presumptuous and downright arrogant to presume that one country, or one city, or one region has all the answers. I agree with you that it's possible to stay true to your core values and beliefs, but I think it's just as imperative that we look beyond our own confines, our own borders, our own day-to-day lives to see what is working in other places. I think the rest of the world has certainly learned from America, how our democracy works, and we've got things we can learn from other countries. To not embrace it is just very foolish. And if people can travel independently, outside of tour groups, they will probably be in more situations where they are exposed to new things, and have an opportunity to learn more. Of course, there are many great tour groups, and I'm not down on them in general, but I think independent travel is the way to go. As you said, actually living abroad is the very best way to immerse yourself in a different experience.

DH: Absolutely. I think it depends on what phase of travel that you're in. I was talking to Tony Wheeler [cofounder of Lonely Planet] for this book a couple of weeks ago, and he said, "I'm in a car outside the Sydney Opera House, and I'm looking at this massive cruise ship. I gotta tell you, I don't get it. But I guess they're traveling." And we had this great conversation about that—if it takes them getting on a gigantic boat in a place that they feel safe, and only experiencing a couple of hours of these different cities, maybe that's just the first step towards them deciding, "Hey, next time maybe we could do this by ourselves. Now that we've had a little taste of it."

CC: I think that's well put, Daniel. Europeans have a great advantage, having so many countries at their doorstep, so to speak, and Europeans are great travelers. They are comfortable with different languages, different cultures. America, being separated by an ocean on each side, we've got Canada and Mexico as our neighbors, but we don't have access to so many small countries and cultures.

DH: Absolutely.

CC: The Japanese are a great example of what you talked about. Years ago, many Japanese only traveled with tour groups. There was always a group of thirty, forty, fifty people marching along, with a tour guide holding a flag up in the air so nobody got lost. Now the Japanese, particularly young Japanese people, have become very comfortable traveling on their own. And they look forward to the cultural experiences. But those who are traveling for the first time or the second time, you're right, it's a comfort zone. And as people get older, sometimes it's easier, more convenient to travel where the arrangements are taken care of by somebody else.

DH: Okay, so fifty countries, that's an impressive list. I'm at like thirty-five or forty. Name a country you haven't been to yet that you're dying to go to.

CC: I've never been to Russia. I've never been to the Baltics. My mother's family actually emigrated to the US from Lithuania, so that's definitely on my bucket list. A lot of my travel over the years has been influenced by where we were doing business, and the ability to tack on leisure time either before or after the business trip. In the later years, much of that was international. So, I've only been to Warsaw, for instance, for a day. I would like to get back to Warsaw. I've never been to India, I would definitely like to get there.

DH: Nice. I've asked this next question of everyone, and I've gotten some pretty interesting answers. Is there a trip you recall where something went horribly wrong? Your flight got canceled, you got unbelievably lost?

CC: Well, maybe not horribly wrong. But one of the funnier things was when my wife and I were traveling with our children, who I think were in their teens. And I've been known to arrive at the airport just in time to catch the plane. I do that for meetings, and I try to cram in as much as possible. So my wife was determined, when we were coming back from a trip to Spain, that we were going to get to the airport in plenty of time. So we got out of bed at five in the morning and packed the night before. I drove to the airport and went to return the rental car. The counter was basically empty. There was nobody there. I smirked to myself, "My wife got us out so early the counter isn't even open yet." And lo and behold, I check the board, and it turns out our flight had left the day before.

DH: Almost the same thing that happened to me! Amazing.
CC: I had changed my connection. I had told her one day for the travel back, and although the ticket had the correct date, the original date stuck in our minds. And there we were, the four of us. The kids had to get back, because Easter break was ending. Fortunately, this was back when things were much less complicated, and we were able to take our tickets to another airline, and they even honored the tickets, which would be hard to imagine today.

There was another time I went to Canada, and I'm ready to do business on July 1. I knew who I wanted to see, and it was an exploratory trip, so I didn't make any firm appointments. But when I went downstairs, the streets were completely deserted. I asked the lady at the counter what was going on and I found out it was Canada Day.

DH: Yeah, it's so close to the Fourth of July.
CC: I'm not sure how I passed the day, but I certainly didn't do everything I wanted to. I've had my briefcases stolen a couple of times—once in Paddington Station, once in Las Vegas. I've had my pocket picked in Italy, lost my wallet. And the same thing happened in Germany. One time in Germany someone actually got my wallet out of my front pocket, which is pretty hard to do. Someone jostled me as we got on the train, and I said, "Hey, what are you doing?" and the guy pushed his way past me, and you know, thirty seconds later, I realized my wallet was gone. I jumped off the train and chased him, but he was way too fast.

DH: Yeah, I've been really lucky. I've never lost a bag. And the only time I've ever been robbed, it was my phone. And I actually got it back before I left the restaurant. There was

a person going around who grabbed three or four different phones in the span of about five minutes. But like you, it's never been anything that would deter me from traveling—just a reminder to be more self-aware.

CC: Yeah, I was in Amsterdam once and I had a duffel bag I had left in my car, it actually had some business files in it. I came back to the car and the window was broken, and the bag and the files were gone. I inquired where the local police station was and walked to it—it wasn't too far away. And I guess someone picked it up, looked into it, found out it only had business papers in it, and abandoned it. Someone else actually picked it up and turned it in to the police station. The same thing happened to me in Tokyo. And the next day I went to the police station, where someone had turned it in. So sometimes these things can end well.

CHAPTER 3

EXPANDING YOUR PALETTE

The Subconscious Effect of Travel

Most of us, by the time we're grown up, have a pretty firm set of preferences: what we like to eat, the type of music we listen to, who our friends are, our politics.

Unsurprisingly, these preferences weigh heavily in where we end up traveling. Can I really ride the Trans-Siberian Railway through Mongolia alone when I know that only 3 percent of people in Mongolia speak English? Can I stomach the kind of food I'm sure I'll get stuck with in India? Will people treat me differently in Russia when they realize I'm "not from around here?"

Unless you're the adventurous type that's obsessed with opening yourself up to new experiences (and we will see, in a later chapter, how travel can become an addiction), you're probably not looking to change *everything* that makes you comfortable—especially when you're supposed to be on vacation.

I grew up in Fayetteville, Georgia, just outside of Atlanta. The best restaurant in town (not counting El Ranchero Mexican restaurant) was Chick-fil-A. You can laugh, but Fayetteville is just a short drive from Hapeville, where Chick-fil-A was founded, and in our town, it was a sit-down restaurant.

I wasn't exposed to exotic foods. I loved chicken nuggets, mac and cheese, and bread, in any form or fashion.

You can imagine my apprehension when I realized I was headed to India and China for the first time—on a business trip. I had never even eaten at an Indian restaurant when I stepped off the plane in Bombay for the first time.

My fear of foreign foods was foolish when I think about it now, but at the time it was very real. What the actual fuck, I asked myself, am I going to eat in these places?

I had heard the horror stories from friends who had been of getting sick—"Delhi belly," endless nighttime vomiting. The day before I left, I drove to REI and bought four dried backpacking meals, basically MREs. I would be ready, no matter what happened.

As usual, I couldn't have been more wrong. Not only was Sesh, the director of our Indian office, a fantastic tour guide, but he was determined not to let me, his boss, get sick on my debut tour of the subcontinent.

He methodically steered me toward and away from various types of food—seemingly without rhyme or reason—as we made our way across India that week. Things I thought I should never eat, like fresh fruit from a street vendor, he would bless with approval, and then refuse to let me drink milk with my cereal at a five-star hotel the next morning.

About three days in, I realized I *loved* nearly everything we had eaten and actually looked forward to our next meal. The backpacker food sat silently in my suitcase, as my preconceived ideas of spicy and overpowering Indian cuisine melted away.

Luckily, I didn't throw away the camp food.

A few weeks later, I had a business meeting in Beijing. I had never been to China before, but if there was one thing I knew I loved, it was Chinese food. I had kept the camping food in my suitcase mostly because I knew the twelve-hour time difference would be difficult to adjust to, and I didn't want to be starving at 3 a.m. with nowhere to find a bite to eat.

The first night I arrived, I turned the hotel room iron upside down and heated up some water, a trick I learned from my mother, and added it to one of the camp meals. I had landed late and didn't want to venture out at midnight. Little did I know, I should have been rationing.

As it turns out, the type of Chinese food we are exposed to in America should really just be called American food, as I didn't find a single thing in common with the native cuisine, other than rice being a theme.

The next night, I had a business dinner with our Chinese counterparts, and after a long-winded tour highlighting the history of their company, through what I can only describe as a museum inside their offices, we were seated for our meal.

Chinese business culture, I quickly learned, dictated bringing as many people as possible from your team, when meeting with foreign business associates. It was exactly the opposite of what I was used to, where most negotiations were done in small groups of only two or three very senior executives.

We were escorted into a large ballroom of sorts and seated at one of the largest round tables I had ever seen. I don't recall there being place cards, but it was apparent where I was supposed to be seated. As the CEO of the visiting company, I was to be the guest of honor, right next to my Chinese counterpart, who spoke very little English, and my interpreter, seated on my other side.

There was a flower arrangement right in front of my plate that was so large, I really couldn't see another soul at the table.

Our CFO, Theo, my personal lifeline who had organized the whole trip, was a few seats away. In celebration of our arrival, a toast was prepared, for every single one of the thirty people around the table. A bottle of some sort of rice vodka was opened, apparently both expensive and high proof.

The only reason I survived the rest of this story was that the shot glasses were half-size.

What followed next was a series of toasts from one individual to another where one person would say something, the interpreter would translate, somewhat poorly, and then the person who'd been toasted would take another shot.

I shouldn't have been surprised that I was toasted first. I was, after all, the guest of honor. A few minutes after my first shot Theo leaned closer to me and said, "Make sure you toast him back; you're supposed to wait a few minutes and then reciprocate the good gesture," which of course I did, resulting in a second shot.

If you're sensing a pattern here, I was toasted no less than five more times in the ensuing forty-five minutes, for a total of twelve shots. They may have been half-size, but that was still plenty for me at 11 a.m.

I didn't fully appreciate it at the time, but it turned out I was lucky to be drunk for what came next.

As the lunch shifted into the first course, the staff brought in, tray by tray, various dishes that they would place on a lazy Susan–type rotating server for the table. The opposite end of the table, where I was seated, was close to the door where the food was arriving from, thus I got to watch as they set each dish down. At this point, the massive flower arrangement was removed.

The other duty of the guest of honor was to be the first person that tasted each item brought to the table. I'll spare you the exact details, but just know it was a wild array of animal organs I either hadn't heard of or wished I hadn't.

Sexual organs were a prominent theme as several variations of livestock came out.

The waitress would announce in the Chinese language what each new dish was, and then my translator would explain. I kept taking the first bite and proudly exclaiming to the table, "Fantastic, thank you so much," dying for it to be over. Unlike the rest of the table, who could merely pass up some of the dishes, I was the taster, so I had to eat at least one of everything.

After the food finally ran out, and a few more toasts were toasted, I was drunk as a skunk. Sitting there in my suit, at 11 a.m. local time, completely wasted.

My Chinese counterpart, who ran the company we were meeting with, had begun to tell some jokes, apparently at my expense. The table kept erupting in laughter and looking at me like I had accidentally shown up without pants on.

I got up the nerve to ask my translator what the joke was about, but he was laughing so hard he couldn't explain it to me in English, other than to say, "Mr. Xen thinks you are very funny."

Luckily, during our negotiation, our CFO—who had avoided most of the drinking games—did all of the talking.

I share those two international food experiences because these days, I'm no longer a mac and cheese–only type of guy. I'll really eat almost anything. From raw fish to rare steak, nothing really bothers me anymore. Which would be a big surprise to my seventeen-year-old self.

I have always loved travel, but I had no intention of broadening my food pallete. It happened as a result of a situation that I had no choice but to participate in, or risk being disrespectful to people who didn't deserve it.

Phil Rosenthal - *Somebody Feed Phil* "Vacation Magic"

Phil Rosenthal is perhaps best known as the creator, writer, and executive producer of *Everybody Loves Raymond* (1996–2005), but these days he's traveling the world as the host of the hit Netflix show *Somebody Feed Phil*. On the show, which has just wrapped filming its second season, Phil takes the viewer on a world tour, eating his way through an endless array of countries.

Daniel Houghton: Phil, tell me a little bit about some of the places you've been and perhaps give us a two-minute overview of the travel show you're making right now.
Phil Rosenthal: The show is . . . me trying to get you to travel by showing you the best places in the world to eat. The way I pitched the show initially was I said, "I'm exactly like Anthony Bourdain . . . if he was afraid of everything."

I figured there were a lot of people like me on the couch, watching Bourdain and marveling at him and what a superhero he was and saying: "He's fantastic. I'm never doing that."

I thought if they saw a schlemiel like me out there, they would say to themselves, "Well, if he can do it, I certainly can do it." And that's the whole point of the show.

The only reason I have to be doing it, the only thing I can offer the genre that Bourdain so brilliantly reinvented, is my own sense of humor. The belief that we all have, that food is the great connector—for me, the laughs are the mint.

DH: Tell me a little bit about when you were growing up. What was your first experience with traveling, going to different places and different countries?

PR: When I first started traveling, I didn't have any money. I was a struggling artist in New York in the early eighties. I'd never been overseas. I've never been anywhere, really. I got a job as a courier for DHL before they had their own cargo planes, kind of like Federal Express. They would send their stuff as your excess baggage, meaning they would have a kid or somebody sit on a plane, like Swissair, in coach, and all their stuff would go as your excess baggage. It was cheaper for them to do it that way.

You would just be in charge of the luggage tags, and you would get off in Zurich, let's say, and give the luggage tags to a man holding a DHL sign. Then you were free to go and explore Europe for two weeks or whatever, they didn't care, they were not paying us. All you got was the coach ticket, but that was all the incentive I needed to go.

So that's what I did. I spent two weeks in Europe, and then I would do the same thing to get home. I did that a couple of times, and I would figure it out so that my friends would take the Tuesday or Wednesday flight to Zurich or to Frankfurt or Brussels, and we would meet up and have those two weeks and then fly back.

And then, I met a girl and did it with her . . . and then I married her because . . . you know, you take a girl to Paris and it kind of seals the deal.

DH: Ha! Indeed.

PR: So that was my first trip. The first time I saw Paris, in 1983, walking around and going, "God, this is so beautiful," I just loved every minute of the day, and I thought, "I've got to remember this, what this feels like." Sure enough, it changed my life and my worldview.

What I mean is, I came back to Washington Heights in Manhattan, and I would walk in the park in Fort Tryon Park near my apartment and look at that and say, "Well, first of all, this is very European!" How do I know? Because I was just there! We have beautiful trees here too! Not just in Paris. But I didn't appreciate it until I had some basis for comparison. Right? That's what travel does, it opens your mind. There's no more mind-expanding thing we can do in the world than travel.

It changes your life. I tell everybody, "Listen, especially today, just you going there and being a half-decent person, not even a fully decent person, you're an ambassador for our country, and it's very, very important that we put that out there. Even more than that, for you, what you get back is, it enriches your whole life. It changes your entire worldview, it changes your whole perspective on the rest of your life. You can't buy that.

DH: With this book, I'm trying to do the same thing, I think, that you set out to do on the show, which is just to show anyone and everyone that this is something that you can do. It's a lot to book that first international trip, and the logistics alone scare a lot of people out of it. My whole point in bringing other perspectives into this book is I want people to know that even people they see like you, on TV, leading them around the world, all of those people had to take their first trip at some point. I just hope you make people book a lot of plane tickets to get out and see the world.

PR: I get such a response, and this is the best thing about the show for me. The people who write to me on Instagram and Twitter and Facebook and tell me that their lives have been changed because they were inspired to travel. That they went to some of the same places and to some of the same restaurants and even ate some of the same dishes that I eat on the show! But more than that, they met the people, and they understood what it is to travel. These are things that make your life better! I can't imagine now a life without travel.

It makes me so happy. This is why I want to keep doing the show forever, because of the gifts that I get back, the knowledge that people's lives are changing, and that it means something to them. Even if they can't travel at that very moment, they understand why it's important.

Something to shoot for, something to save up for. Right?

DH: Absolutely. In all of your travels, what was the place that you went to that you thought you had a pretty good idea what it would be like, and then you got there and it was completely different than what you had imagined? For me, India was that trip. I thought I knew what it would be like. I grew up with people that had moved from India, I had eaten Indian food, but when I got there for the first time, it completely changed every opinion that I had and really took me aback. What's the place that did that for you?

PR: I did some thinking about Hong Kong when you say that. I was expecting kind of a giant Chinatown . . . that's what I was expecting. What I wasn't expecting was an amazing world city. They call it the gateway to the Far East because it's a port of trade, but beyond that, there are influences from all over the world.

You can have an Angelina hot chocolate, from Paris, in Hong Kong. You can't even get that here in New York, although I hear it's coming. But they have everything! The whole city feels so much worldlier than us. Hong Kong, Tokyo. It's mind-blowing.

DH: I couldn't agree more. I went to both last year for the first time and was blown away.
PR: Maybe it was the British occupation for so long, but it's an amazing place. It's fun, the whole place feels like a party.

DH: I went to the Rugby 7's World Cup there last year and was utterly taken aback.
PR: I'll tell you a story, stop me if you've heard it before, but on the first series of *I'll Have What Phil's Having* on PBS, which we filmed in the 1980s. We went to Italy, the first time was on one of those courier trains. I was traveling overnight in the third-class coach cabin from Paris to Florence, and in the cabin with me were these two kids who were my age, a guy and a girl that were dating. We stayed up all night drinking. They told me where to go in Florence and suggested I go to their dad's bakery, so I did! I loved them right away, and I didn't know where else to go.

When I got to that bakery—this was in 1983—the father was so happy to see an American, he looked at me and said, "America! John Wayne!" And he had me sit down at a table just outside the bakery and brought me everything in the bakery to taste.

Then he called his friends next-door from the meat market and the pizza place, and they started bringing me food . . . because I was American. Can you imagine? I was twenty-three years old. I was just a kid. I thought I was like in a Frank Capra movie. I couldn't believe it! I had never been treated like that in my life, so of course, we became lifelong friends.

We lost touch for about twenty-seven years, but then my wife found an address on an old letter. I didn't know where the bakery was anymore; I had moved to LA and started a career in writing and was so enmeshed in that. I hadn't heard from them again. This was pre-internet, pre-everything, and I didn't know how to reach them, until she found that letter.

So we went back, we walked in while we were filming the most recent series and there they were! We had a reunion on the show. We've been back two or three times to see them since.

DH: Share a travel story of a trip when something's not gone according to plan . . .

PR: I've had some things where you want to go to some place specific, but then you get there, and it's closed. Every. Single. Time that has happened, something better, some magical experience has happened where someone will say, "Oh, you're looking for this place," "Oh yes, they closed last week," or "They closed for the season," but "Come over here, be our guest." Things like this happen. Then you meet this family and have a magical time . . . you would never have had it! If you just went to the other place. It's a crazy thing how that works, we call it "Vacation Magic." It's a real thing. You put yourself out there and the world kind of conspires to make sure you have a good time.

I'm sure some tragedies happen, but I haven't had one yet. The worst thing that's happened to me was we were in Saigon filming. I asked if we were finished filming a scene, and I was walking back to the hotel. Like an idiot, I was looking at my phone to figure out how to get home. I wasn't watching where I was going.

A guy on a scooter on the sidewalk came by and snatched the phone out of my hand, and that was that.

DH: Luckily you can always get another phone.

PR: It's the number one crime in the world. I was happy I wasn't hurt, I was happy I didn't turn into the guy and get run over. It's a little frightening, an invasion of your space and a theft, but with just the forethought that you don't walk around with your phone out for people to see. That phone is probably a year's salary for that guy. We take it for granted, how lucky we are. That said, every single other person in Vietnam was so lovely and so welcoming. Have you been there yet?

DH: I haven't! It's been at the top of my list for a while, and I want to get there before the year is over.

PR: Well, *there's* a place you have a certain expectation of what it's like, and then your mind is changed. I talk about it in the Saigon episode, but the only frame of reference I had for Vietnam was the war movies that I grew up watching and the news. So what do I know?

I'm almost like ... afraid to go, like, "How much fun is this going to be?" But everyone who had been before me told me it's their favorite spot. You get there, it's a very young country, and not only do they not talk about the war, but a lot of them were born after the war. They are not fixated on it; they see Americans as tourists and visitors and neighbors even, and it was nothing but the utmost kindness, and that was a wonderful surprise for me.

DH: I want to talk a little bit about how food and travel intersect. It's the premise of your show, but I know a lot of people are watching because you're showing them around the world, but others may be really into food and not that into travel. How do those two things come together for you?

PR: The other thing, in addition to not traveling at all, is I didn't have a lot of delicious food growing up. My parents worked, and great food wasn't a priority. Cheap was the priority, so that's what I got. I remember begging my parents as a kid to go to McDonald's. It was a novelty, and it tasted really good to a kid.

As soon as I left the house and went to college and started experimenting with food, I fell in love with it. Going to Europe that first time, one of the mind-blowing things was how delicious everything was. You meet people over the meal. It's the great connector. It's our social life beyond that. As for how it connects to travel, you're literally taking in the culture!

A lot of people's primary business, especially in the Far East, is food! That's what they do for a living. It doesn't have to be expensive; the street food is some of the best that you will ever have in your whole life, but they figured out how to make a living by making it delicious.

DH: What are some of the things that you try to share with first-time travelers, who may not yet have left the country? You have a fantastic responsibility to show people the world— what goes through your mind when you're filming that?

PR: Well, you see me implore the viewers. If you look at the end of the Venice episode, I devote the entire ending of that show not begging them, but imploring them, to go. You gotta have what I'm having! You have to do this! There's no more mind-expanding thing in the world you can do. We would all be better if we could experience a little bit of someone else's experience. The world is . . . mostly beautiful and we don't even know it because we sit in the house and watch TV and think it's not real! We go to Disneyland, which is a facsimile of the real thing, but you're not seeing the real thing. It's like the difference between kissing a picture of a girl and kissing a girl!

Two-thirds of Americans don't have a passport, did you know that?

DH: I did, but it's still hard to believe. Every once in a while I'll remember and shake my head.
PR: Well, maybe shows like mine can help. There are lots of other wonderful people doing shows, you don't have to look at me! Samantha Brown and Andrew Zimmern—there's tons of these shows around the world.

DH: Thank you so much for making the time, it was great to connect and set this up all through Twitter. I was trying to find your agent and figure it out, but Twitter made it happen!
PR: It's pretty great because we can contact almost anyone, it doesn't guarantee that they will respond, but if you DM people, you might be able to get them!

DH: The open DM on Twitter almost always leads to exciting adventures!

Doug Mills

Imagine having flown over a million miles on Air Force One. Doug Mills has—and witnessed history unfold through his camera—as a photojournalist covering the White House for the last twenty-five years. If you wanted to write a one-sentence summary of his career: He was there when Reagan told Gorbachev to "tear down this wall"; he was in the room (and on the plane) with George W. Bush on 9/11; and just a week before we spoke, he came up in conversation during President Trump's summit with North Korean leader Kim Jong-un, when the president remarked to Kim, "That guy is one of the best photographers in the world."

Daniel Houghton: It's hard to know where to start. I'm lucky to know you and many of your incredible stories, but give me an overview of what travel means for you and your career.
Doug Mills: Obviously, my job consists of nonstop travel. Probably 90 percent of it is presidential travel, traveling around the country and the world with presidents since Ronald Reagan. If it's not going with the president on Air Force One, I'm traveling to sporting events, whether it's the Olympics, summer and winter, golf tournaments, Super Bowls, World Cup, that kind of stuff.

DH: You've been a witness to history more than anyone else in this book, and you have such a unique perspective. When you think back over the years, what are the things that really stick out?
DM: When I started with United Press International and traveled to Geneva to see President Reagan and Mikhail Gorbachev

meet for the first time, being in Cold War Geneva, seeing the world for the first time.

I mean, I was a kid who came from Arlington, Virginia, who had not really traveled abroad at all, or even outside the East Coast. To be thrown into a job and put on a plane and sent to the farthest spots in the world, it was pretty exciting.

I would say, with Reagan, going to Germany, when he told Mikhail Gorbachev, "Tear down this wall," I was there for that historic moment. I also went to the beaches of Normandy with Reagan, Clinton, and Obama. I can't remember going there with Bush. That's the thing, a lot of presidents go to the same countries, right?

That Russia trip was my first trip to Moscow. I was probably in my early twenties, and I landed and went to our local bureau. I got on the subway, and I looked like an alien compared to everybody there. It was 1987, everyone knew I was an American. I had on blue jeans and Converse tennis shoes. They had not seen a lot of Americans.

When the president got there, he talked about the different cultures during the trip with us. He kept talking about the Russian hats everyone wore. He was talking to us on the press corps, asking us if we had gotten one. "Everyone needs one!"

DH: Which presidential trip sticks out the most?
DM: One of the most memorable obviously is being with President Bush 43 on 9/11. It was a day that I'll never forget. We had traveled from Florida to Barksdale Air Force Base in Louisiana to make his first remarks to the country about the attacks. Air Force One was the only airplane in the sky in the entire country. The F16s that were escorting us back were just off the wings of AF1 as we flew back to Andrews Air Force Base.

Before we went to Andrews, we actually flew out to an air force base in Nebraska where the president went into the underground protective bunker. On the way back we made a pass over the Pentagon, which was still on fire. It was a day I'll never forget.

DH: Where have you been with the president recently?
DM: Just last week we went to Vietnam for President Trump's second meeting with Kim Jong-un. I'm sitting there, and the president of the United States is sitting next to Kim Jong-un, and he starts talking about me, telling Kim, "Doug is one of the greatest photographers in the world." I'm standing there thinking, "He's sitting next to the North Korean leader, how is this a topic of conversation? Is this a cultural thing, talking about an American?"

DH: When you think about the two moments you have spent with Kim and President Trump, what was going through your head?
DM: The first meeting, I forgot how young Kim Jong-un was. It just kind of hit me, like, "Wow, look how young he is compared to our president, who's in his seventies, this guy is in his thirties."

The kind of power he has in his country and the influence that he has in a meeting like that—he's speaking for so many people. He actually responded to questions from two US reporters on this trip; we never expected that.

There was a little kerfuffle at the first summit when one of the reporters shouted out something about Michael Cohen [President Trump's former lawyer, then under criminal investigation], which I think the president took offense to and thought it was inappropriate during a meeting like that. They had told us they were going to limit the number of photographers and reporters at the most recent summit.

When Kim Jong-un spoke and said, "I wouldn't be here if I didn't want to denuclearize," we thought, "Wow, this is going to be amazing, right?" Everyone thought it was going to be really positive. We thought they had made great progress. We were expecting they might even have a signing today for them to lift sanctions, and then we found out it wasn't going so well. The press conference moved up two hours, and we found out we were leaving early.

Having two people in the room like that, you realize that you're witnessing history. I was one of only four US photographers in the room alongside four North Korean photographers.... That kind of weighs on you when you think about being there, documenting history.

Everyone's presence in the room is negotiated before we get there, by the White House. We get checked by both US Secret Service and North Korean Police, checking all our equipment. It all makes you realize what a small group of people you're experiencing history with.

DH: When you're in the room and looking at those North Korean photographers, and you realize, "These guys are not too different than me." How strange is it to think about that? I like to think they are good people who just want to have a family and a normal life.

DM: Absolutely. There was a moment during the second summit when the two groups of photographers, us and the North Koreans, were all working on figuring out where we would position ourselves for the photo. They didn't seem to have any interest in going down in front and kneeling down right next to me.

I realized they don't want that perspective. I didn't know it until after the photo op, and we were all sitting there together looking at the images on our laptops. We were all kneeling down up front, and they all came in with their big ladders—there was actually a foot-high riser behind us. They went up as high as they could, and when you look at the pictures, our perspective was head-on, it shows how much taller Trump is than Kim. If you're standing up on a ladder, now you're shooting down from like an eight-foot elevated position, so he doesn't look as short.

During one of the photo ops, a North Korean photographer came up to me and was really pushing on me. He wanted my spot. I thought, "You know what, I'm going to try something different," so I gave him my place. His eyes almost fell out of his head when I told him, "You can take my spot." He was very thankful. Then I asked him if I could borrow his ladder, and he gave it to me, and I made a nice picture.

When I saw him on the second trip, he remembered me. We had this really nice handshake and embrace about it all. He had an interpreter, so we talked a little bit. He couldn't have been nicer, and it was neat to realize he remembered the moment. This is Kim Jong-un's lead photographer, so to have a rapport with him was really amazing. I actually gave him two boxes of M&M's from Air Force One—he was very happy.

DH: Update to the readers: The photographer Doug's speaking about, Mr. Ri, was reportedly fired a few weeks after this interview for breaking the photography rules. He stepped in front of Kim during an appearance, to take a photo, and it blocked the view from others.

DH: How do you think all your travels have changed you as a person?

DM: Traveling is an education every time you land in a foreign country. It adds to your knowledge of the world. So many times we go on these trips, and we are with the president meeting with different leaders, we are googling and finding out more about the country we are about to go to, trying to understand the history.

I just think landing on foreign soil forces you to learn about the country that you're in. Knowledge is power. You're learning more to talk to your children about, so they can look at the world differently.

It's the best thing that can happen to anybody, to have the opportunity to travel to a foreign country and experience different cultures. We are all humans, yet we are all brought up differently.

DH: I always think that if we all had the opportunity to travel the world, we would all be in a better place.

DM: Especially for people that have a narrow view of the world, to get out of the United States and see how other people live, there's nothing more valuable than that. It broadens your whole perspective.

DH: Talk to me about the craziest place you've ever been?

DM: Traveling with the first lady Hillary Clinton when she went on one of her trips to Africa. As a journalist sitting in a lodge in Africa, I went to the team and asked what city we were in as I was writing my caption. "Timbuktu," they said, and I asked again, "No really, where are we?" "Timbuktu." I thought, "Wow." I just laughed. I sat down at a typewriter at the time, and put that on a caption, you know, it was just crazy.

We had schlepped these Halliburtian forty-pound cases with a satellite transmitter around the whole trip. We were only allowed to send one picture, and it took two hours. That's the only picture the world is going to see for now from the trip. Being in a far-off place like that, you realize the cultures of the internet and poverty and how it's just so different than everything you have at home, where I could just plug into a telephone line. Those moments will never, never leave me because it shows how far we've come.

DH: These stories are incredible to hear because I've seen these pictures. I've watched them in real time and noticed your byline. When you send those images, and you're sitting there with a quiet moment, do you think, "I'm the only person that's documenting this, and my picture is going to be how the rest of the world learns about what's just happened"?
DM: It's usually when I see it in print on the front page of the newspaper or in a magazine or something like that. You feel like, so many people have seen this photograph because you were the one that was there.

I was the one that was chosen to be there, I was the one that was lucky enough to be there. Hopefully, I was lucky enough to make the best picture possible to represent what happened.

To me, somebody looks at a picture and thinks one thing, and ten people think something else. You could put out a picture of President Trump, President Obama, President Bush, anybody. Some people will look at it totally different ways, whether it's positive or negative, whether they don't like the politician or whether they don't like the picture, because the politician doesn't fit what they have in their mind. Or they don't think it puts him or her in the best light. You can make a funny picture of President Trump, and 50 percent will love it, and 50 percent will hate it.

DH: Tell us about going to China with President George H. W. Bush.

DM: That trip was when President Bush was newly elected—and it's Bush 41 I'm talking about here. He was ambassador to the United Nations starting in 1971 and chief to the Liaison Office in China starting in 1974. I went on his trip when he returned to visit China as president, and what a fantastic trip it was.

Just to see him get out, you know, around town to places like Tiananmen Square, shaking some hands and standing up on the running board of his car, waving to the people there. You could tell he felt very at home even though we were so far away, because he had been the ambassador. It was just a thing we couldn't relate to, but it was apparent he felt very comfortable there and had many friends there.

DH: And then you went back to China, for the Beijing Olympics decades later?

DM: I did, which was an incredible month, just being in such a controlled environment as the Olympics are, you didn't really get as much of the day to explore the culture like you would if you were there as a tourist because you're a little isolated to that. But we were able to get out a number of times and go into all the neighborhoods, grabbing a taxi to go somewhere and have an authentic meal.

Those are always exciting countries to have a meal in, you know, especially if you travel with a colleague. Chang Lee, one of my colleagues, knew a New York Korean guy who was very adventurous about his food. We would go to a restaurant that he had been to before. They brought us a live fish that was laying there not yet dead, but it's laying there, and you're ready to eat it and have this incredible experience. And then, you know, you gotta eat the ice. That's good luck. And, you know, just things like that. It just, I mean, what travel does to the soul. And what it does to the mind, it does nothing but enhance it.

DH: Do you ever wonder what the presidents are thinking when they are going to new places for the first time?
DM: Absolutely. I wasn't on this trip, but there's a time when President Bush accidentally walked out the wrong door and made a funny face, my friend Charlie made a very famous picture of it.

There are just these moments, you know, when you know the president is thinking, "Okay, yeah, I'm in a strange place just like you guys. I don't know which door I'm supposed to be going through like I know every door at the White House." When you get to a foreign country, they don't. I think every president lands in a foreign country and they are doing the same thing that we are when we're going from the airport to the hotel, or the airport to the event. They are looking out the window and looking at all the people looking at the motorcade, which always is a striking thing to me, no matter what country you're in.

Whether it's in Vietnam or China or wherever it is, there are onlookers, and there are people who are curious about see-ing the American vehicles. When we travel, the government flies over every vehicle in the motorcade. The staff is often riding on a local bus, but the president has his limousine, the war wagon, the Secret Service, all those vehicles are flown over to every trip they go on. They like do to a little sightseeing, just like we do when we land in foreign countries.

CHAPTER 4

EXPECTING THE UNEXPECTED

Riding the Waves of Change

NOVEMBER 21, 2013, CHENNAI, INDIA

I had been in India for a little over a week, on a work trip for Lonely Planet. I was traveling around the country with the head of our India office and found myself in Chennai, in a cab, headed to dinner with Sesh, when I got a notification on my phone.

"Check-in now available for United flight 49 to Newark." I was jet-lagged, exhausted, and hungry. The constant blaring of car horns in India is no joke. We were sitting in standstill traffic, cows crossing the road, the whole nine yards.

I sat there confused, staring at the departure information. I wasn't supposed to take off until tomorrow. Why did my phone say the flight was tonight? I went back and forth a few times between the calendar app on my phone and the United app, until it dawned on me.

I was across the international dateline, and I had misread the day of my departure. I sat there in the cab, double-checking dates with Sesh over and over again. I was supposed to fly from Chennai to Mumbai on Air India to then switch terminals and board a direct United flight back to Newark. At the time, the Newark–Mumbai flight was the longest commercial flight in the world.

Sesh looked at me and said, "Go." He knew I would be able to get a cab back in the right direction, so he took out his wallet, handed me 50,000 Indian rupees, and told the cabdriver to rush me back to the hotel.

Our driver drove me back like a bat out of hell. I swung the door open and took off running up the massive stairway to get to my room. I had around thirty-five minutes to pack my bags and run back down to the cab, drive to the airport which was about a half hour away, get through security, passport control, and get boarded before departure. I never thought I would make it.

I stuffed shit into my suitcase as fast as possible, did the Tasmanian devil tour around the room to try to make sure I had everything, and sprinted back to my cab. I think the driver enjoyed the mission. He drove like a man possessed, and we made it in twenty-five minutes. As we were pulling into the airport, he asked me, "International or domestic?" "International," I quickly responded.

I grabbed my bags from the trunk and darted up to the airport front doors to show my boarding pass. In India, most of the airports have armed guards at the entry, and unlike in most other places around the world, you can't even enter the airport without a boarding pass.

The guard looked at me and said, "You're flying to Mumbai, this is the international terminal." Face palm. In my rush, I hadn't thought through that I was actually flying domestic across India before my United international flight back to the States. He looked at me and then pointed to the right. "The domestic terminal is about a quarter mile down the road, you need to hurry."

Right as I turned around, I saw my cabdriver pull away. There was not a car in sight. I did the only thing I knew to do. Put my suitcase over my head and take off sprinting . . . a quarter mile down the road. The only thing that kept me going was the realization that if I missed this flight, I would be delayed getting home by three extra days.

I was so exhausted when I got to the domestic terminal I almost collapsed. I got into the terminal and ran straight up to the security line and begged the man to fast-track me through.

I didn't even go through security; he just took me to the customs counter and had my passport stamped and then took me through a series of back doors and employee-only areas of the airport, straight to the gate. I stepped on the plane just as the boarding door closed.

I took the last seat in the very back row, the dreaded middle seat. Domestic carriers don't have the same seat width, leg room, or distance between rows as most major global carriers. I had to sit so far back in the seat to fit that the headrest stopped just below my shoulder blades and my knees were jammed into the seat in front of me.

Being six-four is fantastic at concerts and during a game of basketball; on an airplane, it's a curse.

I was so exhausted from running and rushing for the last forty-five minutes I kept drifting off to sleep, but as soon as I did my head would drop and I would wake up. It was a dark and unusual type of travel hell I was stuck in . . . for the next several hours.

By the time I got to Mumbai and made it on my United flight, where I was thankfully seated in business class, I passed out and can't recall a single detail of the fifteen-hour-and-forty-five-minute flight.

I've taken over five hundred flights in the last eight years, and never once actually missed a plane. That was the closest I've ever come, and I hope it never happens again.

The logistics of travel can scare the shit out of people. You don't hear people talk about it, but travel is hard. There's no class in high school to teach you how to book a flight, schedule a cab, or exchange currency.

When people do get up the courage to put all of those things aside and make their first international trip, the last thing they want is for anything to go wrong. No one wants to miss a flight, stay at a shit hotel, have a bad meal, or get pickpocketed.

Traveling can be intimidating, especially to people who didn't grow up doing it.

Lynda Lloyd

Lynda Lloyd is one of the longest-tenured flight attendants at Delta Air Lines. She's traveled well over 10 million miles, making all of our time with her at forty thousand feet safe and as enjoyable as possible. She made cocktails for Elvis when he bought out the first-class cabin in the 1970s, and is finally retiring after fifty-five years in the air.

In 2018, while CEO of Lonely Planet, I was flying from Atlanta to Stuttgart, Germany, to visit our German partners. When I boarded the flight, there was a note sitting in my seat which read:

"Welcome Daniel Houghton, Delta 360 / Diamond Medallion.

The entire Delta Family appreciates your business & loyalty to Delta. Thank you.

On a personal note, your father—Danny—got me down the BEST run of my life at Telluride—The Plunge. We spent many years skiing the world together & your mom Jean is the best."

Daniel Houghton: Lynda, it's so wonderful to have you as a part of this book. To start, maybe just spend a few minutes telling us about who you are. I'd love to hear how you grew up and why you chose to work in the travel industry.
Lynda Lloyd: I was working for Fifth Third Bank in Cincinnati. That's where I was born. One of the guys that worked there just got a job with Delta. And he said, "You really should interview with them."

Well, I went to the library and I checked out the two airlines—Delta and Eastern—and Eastern had more flights into Cincinnati, so I went and interviewed with Eastern. When I came home and told my father I got the job, he said, "You're not going to be a flight attendant."

The next day, Eastern Flight 304 crashed into Lake Pontchartrain, and shortly thereafter, Eastern went under. Six months later, I was hired by Delta. I was so fortunate.

DH: Did you travel when you were growing up? What made you want to work for the airlines?
LL: No. It was absolutely my dream. I was a cheerleader, all through junior high and high school, and my cheerleader coach was an American flight attendant, and every summer my stepbrother would fly to visit his father in Detroit and I would go to the airport. It's like I said, "If I could just take one trip, just one flight, I'd just be so blessed." And I wound up with the opportunity to fly the world with Delta.

DH: That's amazing. Do you remember how old you were when you took your first flight?
LL: Yeah, my first flight with Delta was from Atlanta to Detroit. A ten-stop Conair 440. It was two engines, a propeller. I never thought I would ever get to Detroit, and when I finally got there, I was so scared because the crew kept knocking on the door and asking me if I wanted to go out to eat and I said, "No, I don't want to go out. I want to sleep." I was scared. I didn't know how crews interacted with each other. So that's where it began.

DH: I want to talk a little bit about what that was like—in the early part of your career. But before we do that, tell me a little bit about how many years you've been at this, what your seniority is with Delta. Any travel stats that you have now that you're decades into this career.

LL: I will have been with Delta for fifty-five years on April 27. I'm having a huge celebration in Atlanta at a very well-respected, beautiful facility. Lots of air and windows. It's, it's where ladies go for lunch. And I have thirty people coming, along with my supervisor.

DH: How many countries do you think you've been to? Any kind of general stats of your career that you can think of?

LL: Okay, I have a map in my den, and my husband and I got it to put down every place we've been. Seventy-seven countries.

DH: Wow.

LL: The only place we haven't been is Antarctica. My husband saw it the other day and he wants to go. I'm more interested in going to this little place that I heard about from another flight attendant called San Sebàstian. It's in the Basque region. And he said it is just absolutely awesome. We watched Rick Steves [travel show host and guidebook author] yesterday, and he was there. He went to this restaurant called Rack? Rec? Anyway, it's just one of those restaurants you have to go that is about an hour from San Sebàstian.

This year we're going to England and Scotland. My husband has never been to England or Scotland, so I wanted to give him that opportunity. And then the next month, we're going to go say goodbye. He's from Germany. He's from the Rhine Gaul region and so we're going to go say the farewell tour to our friends and family all over Germany, Munich, Stuttgart, the Rhine Gaul, and Düsseldorf. That's June. Then in September we're going to Iceland. In October, we're going to San Sebàstian, and then my final trip will be the end of October, a four-day to Stuttgart. I retire November 1, and I am absolutely ready.

DH: Talk to me about how your job has changed since you first stepped on an airplane fifty-five years ago. How has the role of a flight attendant evolved over the years?
LL: Constant change. I've been a leader, I would say, for forty years. Sometimes it was in the second B position. And sometimes it was in the A position. Now they call it purser, the A, and our service leader is the B.

DH: So for people that don't know anything about that, and they just see all the flight attendants, give me a quick overview of how the responsibilities are split up for the flight attendant crew, say on an international flight where there are eight or nine flight attendants.
LL: Well, this airplane that we're flying this month to Stuttgart, this will be my eighth trip in a row on Sunday. And I'm seventy-five years old, so I'm getting really tired of going every Sunday. And thank God I got some time off before my fifty-fifth anniversary visit, because two days later, we're leaving for London.

So the responsibilities of the flight attendants depend on who's working which aisle. Obviously all of us have to check our emergency equipment, to make sure everything's in compliance. And then this last trip, I was a line flight attendant because they took my trip away from me because I didn't bid enough. It was a long trip.

We had a medical emergency on board because there was a man who was diabetic and he drank too much. And he passed out in the back of the airplane and thank God we had four FAMs with us (federal air marshals). One of the FAMs was a medic, so he was there, and there was a nurse that volunteered also. That was really wonderful because he was really in bad shape. I could see his eyes and I knew he was ready to pass out. And sure enough, he did—and hit the emergency slide in the back of the plane that's attached to the boarding door. We had to prop up his legs and call for help. Fortunately, that FAM and the nurse volunteered.

When I get on the airplane as a purser, I deliver a welcome card to each passenger, and then I think I gave you an individual card. Those that sit up front in the business class get an individual card.

What you do on the ground really depends on where you are in the world. In the air, we have two teams working in the back that need to stay together, you know, as they go down the aisle, they need to stay together so they're doing the same thing to each row. The back, where we're doing the drinks, and then the salad, appetizer, entree, and then the dessert cart. Then I get the bedsheets ready for the flight attendants to take their crew rest. I have to take care of the pilots to make sure that they're set. When the pilots have to switch out, I have to make sure that the area is clear, and nobody's walking through the cabin, especially up at the front, so that they don't have access to that door.

Now they've changed the FAMs' situation; they used to be two in the front and two in the back. Now there's only one in the front, which makes no sense. That guy can't sleep. They used to trade off. I don't know if it was a money decision because they take two seats, but it's the way it is now.

DH: Share a couple of stories with me about interesting, wacky, or unusual things that have happened while you've been in flight.
LL: I flew to Las Vegas for years. Elvis Presley performed every night there, and he would leave tickets for us at the desk.

DH: That's fantastic. You had him on your flight?
LL: I had him on the flight. He bought the whole first-class cabin. And he got on the airplane and we took off, and one of his friends came to me, he said Elvis would like to talk to me up in the front lounge. So we sat up there and I sat across from him and he started telling me the story of Priscilla, his first wife. He was going to ask her to marry him.

DH: Was he a good guest to have on the airplane?
LL: Oh, he was such a sweet man. He said to me, "You don't like that uniform you're in, do you?" And I said, "Absolutely not!" It was a base top and we had brown skirts. An unbelievably ugly uniform.

DH: There's been some interesting choices over the years. And there's been some fantastic ones. It's kind of an odd thing. Every few years, when the uniforms would change, my mom would either rejoice or complain.
LL: Yeah. I'm not wild about the purple. It's certainly better than some uniforms we've had. We had what they called the prison guard. They were really horrible. Anyway, it was the most

amazing experience to have Elvis on the airplane. He eventually bought Delta's Convair 880 and painted it black. He was beautiful, though. I mean, those eyes and smile and that little smirk of his. Oh, my God. Ha ha.

DH: He sounds like a charming guy.
LL: He was just a really down-to-earth guy. And all the flight attendants that worked out of Memphis said he was so generous, he would just go up to a guy and get him a Cadillac, a pink Cadillac. That was the kind of guy he was, he would do anything for anybody. And he did. You know, he made lots of money, spent lots of money, but he got into drugs, and that was his downfall.

DH: It's so unfortunate. The guy lived one heck of a life, that's for sure.
LL: Oh, he did. He did. People so admired him.

DH: Travel intimidates a lot of people, so I'm trying to have people share a scary story or something that happened to them. What I found is that a lot of the bad things that happened really aren't that bad. Have there been any scary situations in flight or anything, over all those years that made you go, "Oh, my gosh, I can't believe this is my job"?
LL: Knock on wood, nothing. Just the turbulence is getting more and more and more. All the storms that we have to go from west to east, constant, constant turbulence, and we have to work in that. And we have to decide whether or not we shouldn't work in it. That's hard because it changes, you know—you think it's gonna be okay when you get out of the jump seat, and then it's not.

DH: And then suddenly you have food and drinks flying through the cabin.

LL: And carts. Heavy carts that could get away from you and hurt somebody. That's something I can't wait to get over when I retire. I'm ready to spend my time in my garden and actually enjoy traveling for pleasure.

DH: What would you say to nervous fliers? I always try to tell people, it's hard to believe, but those airplane wings can go up and down forty-something feet before they snap. The plane is a lot more flexible and durable than you think. But what do you say? I'm sure you've had to do this many times in your career, calm people down.

LL: You really have to be emphatic about checking seat belts, because even the best traveler forgets. I go through and make sure every person has their seat belt on. I tell them you have to tighten it because the airbags in the front cabin, we have airbags in those seat belts. So if you fasten it just a little bit, the airbag won't help you. You can tell there's so many of them that just are so nonchalant about not having their seat belts fastened during the flight, and then right before we land, they can't find their seat belt because the seat belt has gone under the seat. And of course, I have to make them get out of the seat so I can move the seat back and get the seat belt out. The average traveler, they really should not be concerned about the air travel. It's the safest form of transportation in the world. Look at the car crashes you see on TV. I saw one just yesterday; there was a school bus that was hit by a great big truck and there was a car in the middle. The person in the car was killed. You can't beat air travel, it's so much safer than driving. Luckily, nobody was injured on the school bus.

DH: You know, I think the thing about seat belts is that a lot of people think, "Well, I only need this if the plane crashes," but the truth is, it almost has nothing to do with that. It's really about keeping you from flying about the cabin or keeping you in place. You know, if a drink glass goes flying and pops you in the head.

LL: We've been lucky. I've been lucky, because I heard of an airplane recently that landed because they got hit by lightning. Then I think there was recently also an airplane that had several people that had to go to the hospital, one of them was a flight attendant. So people are too nonchalant, say about their seat belts, and they can be severely injured if they're thrown into the ceiling.

DH: Absolutely. And then you're stuck in the, as my mom would say, the Coke can for the next several hours until you get to a hospital somewhere.

Talk to me about the best tips or advice you have for people flying. You watch thousands of people a week dragging all this luggage on planes. Are there funny stories from that? My mom tells a story of flying to the Caribbean in the seventies and people putting chickens in the overhead bins.

LL: I was on a trip to San Salvador once and they were bringing on microwaves.

DH: Oh my goodness, and putting them in the overhead bin?
LL: Unbelievable. Yes.

DH: How has the industry changed over the years? You've been through many CEOs, leaders, and good and bad times.
LL: Our best CEO was Richard Anderson [Delta CEO from

2007 to 2016]. He was amazing. He gave me my forty-five-year pin. I wrote him a note telling him that I got my orchid from C. E. Woolman when I graduated from training fifty-five years ago. I said to him, I know that you have commissioned C. E. Woolman's desk for your office, and since I got my orchid from him, I would really like to see the desk. He invited me to come meet him in his office, and that's where he found the book *Rules of the Road*, which was written by C. E. Woolman.

DH: For those of you reading, C. E. Woolman was one of the founders of Delta Air Lines. It's amazing you've been working since he was still handing out orchids to new crew members.
LL: Richard led the airline by always remembering what it was like to sit on the other side of the desk. Treat people like you want to be treated, and that's really what it was. I was selected to go to the fortieth anniversary of Delta being in Atlanta. I was onstage with Richard Anderson, the chairman of Coca-Cola, the governor of Georgia; the woman sitting next to me had done the most builds for Habitat for Humanity, and then the gentleman next to her was a Delta customer who had seven million miles flown on the airline. He had met his wife, a Delta flight attendant, on a fifteen-minute flight from Knoxville to Atlanta. She works quick.

DH: Yeah, he did something right.
LL: So Richard did a video of me that they played on the screen. There were two thousand people there. I just went through a little bit of my career. And Richard said, "I have something special planned for Lynda." And he went backstage and he came back out with a great big, huge orchid corsage. He said, "I want to complete the circle."

DH: Oh, wow. That's incredible.

LL: Yeah. So that's the kind of man he was. I had an interview with the *Wall Street Journal* guy that day, and he said, "He's not going to be any different [of a CEO] than any of the rest." And I said, "You are wrong. And you can call me back anytime and I will tell you the same thing. This man is for real. He cares. He wants to make this company great again." And sure enough, the guy called me back. And I said the same thing. And he said, "I guess you've been proved right."

DH: That's amazing. You know, not specific to travel, but it is unusual, especially these days, for someone to spend their career pretty much at one place, and I think it doesn't happen a lot anymore. And I think, unfortunately, part of that is because companies don't have the same dedication to their employees that they used to. But also, capitalism works pretty well, and people switch jobs, and you can't blame them for that. When you reflect back on fifty-five years, and you realize that's all with the same employer, what comes to mind for that? That's a pretty remarkable achievement.

LL: Well, I just feel blessed that I was able to have the opportunity to do what I love—fly to all these places, as an attendant, and also as a traveler . . . and it's all due to Delta. I would never have had this opportunity if I had not chosen this company at this time of my life. And I will ever be grateful. And they're so wonderful. The head of all the flight attendants just sent me a note saying that she wants to take me to lunch before I retire. And I said, "Here's my employee number, you can look at my schedule, and we can schedule some time in August to get together." I've known her since she started. And she started out, you know, in the office, behind the desk. I don't know that she flew, but I'm sure she flew for a little bit of time. But she's risen to the top of the list and God, she's wonderful. She's a real person. We have real people working for Delta. That's the important thing to remember. Ed Bastian [current Delta CEO] was trained by Richard, but Ed was the CFO first.

A fun quick story: A girlfriend of mine who just retired last year was number one [in seniority]. She had Ed Bastian on one of her flights. They were coming back from, I think it was Venice. He was on the aisle and she was by the window. He was working away, throwing these papers on the floor. Finally she said to him, "A clean row is a happy row."

DH: That's amazing.
LL: And he said, "Oh, I'm sorry, I'm sorry, I'll clean up." Then one of the flight attendants went by and said, "Hey, Ed, how you doing?" And he said, "You obviously work for Delta?" And she said, "What was your first clue?"

DH: That's amazing.
LL: And he said, "I'm the CFO." And she said, "No, you're not. He's CFO, she's CFO. We bring in the money. You spend it."

DH: What do you feel you've learned about yourself while you've been on the ground in some of these other countries? What do you want to share with people who haven't been anywhere yet, or are just starting to travel? What things had the biggest impact on you, when you think back?
LL: Well, when people ask me, it is truly amazing to me, the number of flight attendants who do not take the opportunity to travel

outside of their job. I am always amazed. When somebody asks me where they should go, I say New Zealand. It's the most incredible. I mean, Sydney is awesome too, but New Zealand is so eye-opening, especially if you do it on the ground, you know. We did a semi-tour of the island. They booked the places for us. Our first trip, we went from Sydney to the Great Barrier Reef, and then Port Douglas. When we got our car and drove out of the parking lot, the driver wound up driving right back where we started. The taxi drivers that were watching us just started laughing.

DH: That's fantastic. Sometimes getting lost is the best part of the trip.

LL: I went over to them and I said, "How do we get to Port Douglas?" because I had planned this trip so that we could do it during the day. Because it's a beautiful drive along the coast. They had a once-in-sixty-years sandstorm the day we were supposed to leave. And Qantas was so wonderful. They went around the airport and gave everybody a bottle of water. And we sat there for eight hours before we left. So we wound up driving at midnight to get to our hotel, which was about two hours away. So I asked them, "How do we get to Port Douglas?" and they said, "No problem, turn right, nine traffic lights and follow the road and you'll get there." I said, "Thank you very much."

DH: Oh yeah, this is the person that's supposed to be getting you there and you're having to give him the directions.

LL: Anyway, that's my favorite place. And we're going to go back again, because we just loved it. Nothing like it. And you have to be on the ground; you have to drive. You have to see the countryside. Don't just fly between places. You have to see the land.

DH: So with seventy-seven countries on the map, what is one of those places that you went to and when you got there it turned out to be different than you expected?

LL: I feel that way every time I go somewhere. Every place I've been, it's been awesome. I wouldn't trade any of them. The Adriatic—wonderful. Scandinavia—fantastic. St. Petersburg—the Venice of the East. I never in my wildest dreams thought I could be in Russia. Everywhere you pick is wonderful. Dubrovnik. Amazing.

DH: I haven't been there, and I really want to go.

LL: Oh my gosh. I mean, really, Croatia. The people are amazing. It's beautiful. The food is great. I wouldn't trade any city I've been to; they've all been fascinating. Except a handful in South America. I've been to Buenos Aires as a flight attendant, and I will never go there again. I've been to Lima as a flight attendant, and I will never go there again. Our crews were attacked twice in the last month. And the last time, the security guard was shot. So they finally got the message and moved us to a different hotel.

DH: I've had mixed experiences in Peru. Mostly fantastic, but I've gotten food poisoning a few times.

LL: My last trip to Buenos Aires, it was eleven o'clock in the morning, I had my pajamas on and hotel robe and my socks. And I heard the boiler blow right outside my room. Boom, bang! And they immediately said to evacuate the hotel. Oh, gosh. And so we were out of the hotel for eight hours—transferred from point to point. And all I had on was my socks, my pajamas, and the hotel robe. It was horrid. And they had a gas leak so we couldn't go back and get our bags. And that was my last trip.

DH: The only time I've ever been booted from a hotel like that was in London, in 2012. There was a fire alarm in the middle of the night; it was at the Marriott over there by the London Eye that used to be a big government building. If there had actually been a fire, it would have been horrible because there are like three exits in the whole damn building.

I'll never forget, it was the night of the Super Bowl, so it was obviously freezing. We got evacuated at three in the morning. I thought it was a real fire. You have to at least pretend like it could be, so I always have a bag by my bed with my passport and cell phone and stuff like that. I think we were out there for three or four hours, and there was no other place to go in the middle of the night in London. Everything was shut.

LL: I think it's a very good plan to have an evacuation kit, your ID or your passport, your cell phone. The important things.

DH: Yeah, I keep a little bag on my nightstand. That's a little collapsible one that I keep in my carry-on. And before I go to bed every night I make sure all of those things are in there because you never know when you're going to have to grab that thing and get out for one reason or another, literally.

LL: Absolutely. Been there, done that!

Fred Dixon

Fred Dixon was raised in the travel industry. As a kid, he started working at his family's hotel in Tennessee, and he has ascended to CEO of NYC & Company, the tourism board of New York City. We spoke about the challenges and opportunities that come with making NYC & Company an example for tourism boards across the world, and he reflected on how he's applied what he's learned from his own travel to one of the most famous travel destinations on earth.

Daniel Houghton: Many people think of New York as the foremost city of the world. How did you find yourself leading NYC & Company?

Fred Dixon: It's an interesting story, because as you may know, my family has a small hotel in Gatlinburg, which my mom still manages. So when we were kids, that was the center of the world for us. Because everyone came together, all of our far-flung family from Virginia. My uncle came from Nashville, everyone came to Gatlinburg, and we all stayed at the hotel, we were all there together. So it really was "ground zero" for my family in every way.

When I was little, we lived there full-time. So, we were having dinner in the apartment in the back, and the buzzer would ring. One of us would have to get up and rent a room or show a room or deliver towels, you know, whatever the case may be. So it's in our blood, you know, hospitality and tourism. This is the world that we've grown up in. And still, to this day, it's a source of income for my family. So it's kind of wild to think I've followed that path all the way to New York. It's been a huge honor. I came here in 2002, I had the pleasure of working for Butch Spyridon [president and CEO of the Nashville Convention & Visitors Corporation] in Nashville—I learned a tremendous amount from him.

Three years after moving to the city I joined NYC & Company, which was my ultimate goal. So I kind of felt like the dog that caught the car. I was really fortunate to be able to move to New York, and then to work for the organization that I had always dreamed of working for. Then in 2014, I was tapped to be the new CEO. So I'm going into my sixth year with that title.

In this role, it's been an amazing journey. And the destination continues to grow, as you know, in really dynamic ways. So we've really endeavored to take on some new narratives, many in line with what you're talking about, in terms of the power of good that comes from travel and tourism. In a city like New York, it really helps us battle inequality, in many ways, and it does unite people and build relationships, across borders, across incomes, lifestyles. New York is a crossroads like no other. In that sense, it is a microcosm of a lot of those ideas that I think you're looking at.

DH: Talk to me a little bit about how New York itself has changed since you got there in 2002. That's a pretty defining period after what happened on 9/11. You've had the opportunity to see the city radically transformed since then. Talk to me about what that's like. Not just as the CEO of that organization, but just as someone that lives there.

FD: The city changed dramatically, in many ways, after 9/11. It was unspeakable in many ways, what happened here. But it did change, I think, our appreciation for each other as humans. The city, there's no question, moves at a rapid speed. The pace of life of everyday New Yorkers is a driven one, you know, you almost have to be a type A personality to make it here to begin with. What 9/11 taught us was that we have to slow down and appreciate each other a little bit more. So I think, as a result of that, the city is a friendlier place than it's ever been before—I think New Yorkers would go out of their way to help you ... all you have to do is stop and ask them. So I think, from a spiritual place and humanist place, I think the city is better.

I think that also, from a global perspective, the city has come back stronger than ever. It's been a beacon to the world in many ways. I can't tell you how many requests we've had throughout the years to travel the world to attend conferences, to speak to communities about that recovery story and what it meant. It is a symbol of resilience for many people, and a story that just keeps unfolding. We're just now finishing the final pieces of the New World Trade Center, with the new Ron Perelman Performing Arts Center going into place.

Barbra Streisand is chairing their board and raising all the money. It's going to be a remarkable new facility. The revitalization of Lower Manhattan, generally speaking, is an amazing story to itself. So the city has come back, you know, really stronger and better, I think, not just spiritually, but also physically, financially. Speaking of the power of tourism—the notion of patriotic tourism, at least in America, was really reborn on 9/11. When the president and the mayor and others said, "What can you do to support New York? You should go there. You should support the community." And we saw that same idea play itself out across natural disasters, terrorist attacks, you know, other tragedies across the years.

Since then, this notion that tourism can be a way to inject, you know, human support for community and also economic stimulus has really caught on, and I think it continues to reverberate and you see that in other cities around the world. Not that New York is trying to take credit for it. But you see, like, certainly in Europe, you see what's happened with the recovery times after some of these horrible terrorist incidents, it's gotten shorter and shorter.

I think people are becoming more resilient, and they also realize that you need to return to these communities to support them and that we can't let the bad guys win. So it's an amazing story of resilience in the city. I think it's stronger today than it was almost twenty years ago.

DH: What is it that you want people to know when they first touch down in New York City? Many people are visiting for the first time, and may have grown up in some other country watching TV shows set in New York, so they have an idea of what it's like.

FD: You actually use a lot of our talking points. For me, coming from a small town, the first time I came to New York, I felt like I had been like plugged into an electric socket. You really feel alive, in many ways, for the first time. And it's interesting because this is a narrative that everyone shares, this notion of New York as a rite-of-passage destination. There are few cities left in the world that really continue to resonate in that same way—New York is definitely one of them. Kids all over the world grow up hearing about New York in songs, reading about it in books. So everyone has a sense of what New York is, and it does represent something different to almost everyone.

Even those of us that live here often forget the role that the city plays in the world. We take that very seriously at NYC & Company, caring for the brand and polishing it. Leadership is an important aspect of our brand, making sure that New York stands out, and for good reasons. A lot of my traveling time is spent speaking at conferences, talking about the power of tourism and why it's so important.

There's no better example than New York of a place where everything is possible, and everyone has an opportunity. It's a city where everyone is treated equally—you've got billionaires standing next to sanitation workers on the subway. It is a city that really just blends, I think, the best of humanity in every possible way. Today it's grown into even more of a multicultural story, given the growth of experiential travel.

DH: I couldn't agree more.
FD: Folks wanting to travel out into the neighborhoods. The city is so multicultural, getting out and exploring—whether it's Flushing Meadows and the Asian community, or Jackson Heights and the Indian community, or whether it's the Afro-Caribbean community and Flatbush—people are getting out and exploring these different cultures and foods. The power of culinary tourism.

My mom has a cousin who is a schoolteacher in Ohio. I don't know her that well because she's always lived in Ohio. But I'd see her at our family reunions or what have you, and I had no idea that she was such a big fan of New York. On summer break, for years, she and her girlfriends would come to New York. Last time I saw her, I said, "So what's your plan this year?" and she said, "Well, we picked two new neighborhoods and two new cuisines." She has spent the last thirty years exploring a different neighborhood every trip.

DH: Wow, and probably never really running into the same thing twice.
FD: Yeah, never running into the same thing twice. It's remarkable how many people really "get" the richness of the texture of

New York, even if they make their home somewhere completely different. So to me, that was just such a powerful story. I just can't help but think that there are so many people like her that we don't even realize are coming here all the time.

DH: Absolutely. Let's talk a little bit about your travel. Give me a little overview of some of the places you've been. What are some things that have stuck out, and just tell me a little bit about you as a traveler?

FD: Sure. I just got back home last week. We stopped in Paris and Hamburg on the way in to talk to presidents about the monumental year that we're having in New York, and all the new developments. There's so much going on—MOMA's expansion, the South Street Seaport district, new Statue of Liberty Museum—it goes on and on and on. New and exciting things happening, and World Pride is coming to New York this year, which is a huge moment for us.

Pride was born in New York. The very first march happened on the one-year anniversary of Stonewall. So now it's gone all around the world, and it's coming home to New York this year. So that's a big story line for us on the team.

But two weeks ago, I was in India, we led a mission there. We go just about every year, to India, because it's a growing market for us—about four hundred thousand visitors coming from India to New York every year. And for me, personally, it's one of my favorite places on the planet. I can't explain it . . . when I was a little kid, I was totally obsessed with India, and I remain obsessed to this day.

DH: I am as well.

FD: Yeah, it's just remarkable in every way. I've been fortunate to visit every continent except for Antarctica. It's on my bucket list.

There's a lot of the world left out there that I want to discover, particularly in South America and Africa. Travel is something I do for a living, but it's also something that I really enjoy doing almost more than anything in my personal life. It's just had such a profound impact on me. I think I wouldn't do my job today if it weren't for this insatiable curiosity that I have about the world. You know, it's interesting, growing up in Tennessee—and I'm sure you've had the same experience—you meet some folks who say, "Oh, New York, I don't need it. I've never wanted to go there." I've never been one of those people.

In some ways, I'm kind of envious of them being happy. But I have been a rolling stone since I was a kid. And this sort of unending desire to learn and discover and meet new people and see new things—it never gets old.

DH: When you think about places that you really want to go, what is it that excites you most? For me, my background is in photography, so it's always like, "I want to see this place; I just want to see it and walk around in it for other people." For some people it's food, or nightlife. What aspects get you the most excited as a traveler?

FD: Yeah, that's a great question. For me, I think it is the cultural bit. I'm fascinated by how other people live. I think one of the great things about my job is when Mayor Bloomberg expanded operations in 2006, he gave us some additional funding, and he said, "Go out and grow the international markets, because they have such a great economic impact on New York." We went out and opened sixteen international offices in a quick two-year time span, and built these relationships with agencies on the ground, and with the press, to really get the sense of the people.

You know, you can make great friends around the world by understanding and appreciating how people live, and the challenges that they face. I'll never forget Moscow for the first time when we opened—we were the only US destination to have a full-time team based in Moscow for years.

DH: Wow.

FD: And we ended up closing the office when it became unsafe there, several years ago. But, you know, I'll never forget meeting people in Russia and learning about their story. They're humans, just like us. They had the Cold War stories that you think you've heard a million times, but seeing how they live, visiting their homes, meeting their friends—you realize that we are all the same.

DH: And that's it. That's exactly why I'm writing the book. I want it to be possible for all of us to have those opportunities. You and I have led very fortunate lives, to be able to be in situations like that. But, especially living in Tennessee, I run into people all the time that have never been on an airplane, haven't left the state or the country. What would you want to say to someone—say, a high school senior who didn't have the desire, was just not curious and didn't know why they should travel? What would you try to shake into them?

FD: I'm going to encourage them to step out of their comfort zone. I mean, I think that's a lot of it. I was fortunate as a kid to be in the marching band, and we traveled a lot, to perform and compete. So it was second nature to me to get on the bus and go somewhere, but a lot of my family did not travel. So even though I couldn't really picture reaching far-flung destinations, I still had the urge. But for a lot of young people, I think they just lack curiosity.

DH: I think some of them feel like, especially with everything on the internet, they can kind of dive into a place, almost as deep as they want, in a way that I don't think either of us knows. Obviously, we didn't grow up with things like that, but I think that gives some people kind of a false sense of feeling that they know what's out there.

FD: I think that's very true. And I think that plays an increasing role, you know, sort of, in the way people view the world, but there's no substitute for human touch. I'm sure that's what this book is going to bring out—the notion that you have to go and see and smell and taste and hear and experience other cultures and how other people live, and the struggles that they face, but also the joys that they celebrate. It's just an incredibly rich world out there, and once that barrier is broken down, it never goes back up.

DH: Right.

FD: We see this in developing markets around the world—the biggest indicator of the potential for a travel market is the growth of the middle class. Because it's human nature to want to explore, and once you have the funds to do it, the first thing you're going to do is explore regionally. And then you're going to eventually be able to travel the long haul to a place that you have always dreamed of going. For many people that's LA, it's Paris, it's Shanghai. Once you taste it, you always want more.

DH: I want you to tell me a story of travel gone horribly wrong for you, maybe one that's a little lighthearted and not too sad. But I'm trying to allow people to understand that even for people that travel constantly, these things go wrong, and

everything's okay. **Is there one story that you're like, "Wow, that was spectacularly nuts"?**

FD: Gosh, yeah. So many stories like that. I'm trying to think of one of the best ones. We had amazing adventures and mishaps in India. We had one day where we wanted to go to the Taj Mahal. You gotta do it, right? We had one afternoon and we said, "Is it possible to get to Agra from Delhi today?" And the very first trip was before the big rings were built for the Olympics. Still not easy to get to. We went through little towns and villages. And when you cross the border from one state to another, you have to stop at a checkpoint and the driver gets out. And I remember the car got surrounded by street performers, with the cobras in baskets and monkeys on leashes.

DH: And you're like, "Is this straight out of a movie?"

FD: Yeah, are we being punked right now? Is this really happening? We did not get out of the car. But it was one of those just totally immersive experiences. We were so out of our comfort zone, we didn't know what to do, but you could tell it was nothing new to the driver. He just said to stay in the car, and we just listened to it. But it was an amazing experience. And I'll never forget that day.

And to return to Russia for just a moment, I remember landing for the first time in Moscow. We had just opened our office in Sweden, and the next morning, we flew to Moscow to open the office there and host an event with the trade and the press. Robert, who ran the agency that did work for us in Moscow, picked me up at the airport. Robert is a storyteller.

He was so proud to work with us. He loved the idea of New York. And he put on—I'll never forget this—Dire Straits on the radio and then we drove—he kind of sped actually, because I remember being a little bit terrified—sped through the streets of Moscow at night, when the Kremlin lit up and around all the sights that you see in movies and hear about, right, I remember just being overwhelmed by how beautiful it was. And I kept pinching myself, and like, is this really happening, and we're really in this car with this Russian that is now working for us, driving through the streets of Moscow at night, listening to Dire Straits and seeing the city for the first time.

The human connection—you can't experience that through a computer. It's these exchanges that make our fears go away. They make us all better people. So, I'm glad you're doing this book.

CHAPTER 5

LIVING SPONTANEOUSLY

Get Rid of the Guidebook

When was the last time you decided to go somewhere and headed to the airport that day?

Have you ever done it? I hadn't until this year.

I was sitting around the house working on writing this book, and the polar vortex was coming. I live in Nashville, so the temperature isn't normally terribly cold in the wintertime. It's a fantastic place to live for a lot of reasons, but the fact that we have four actual seasons is pretty sweet. Growing up in Atlanta there was summer, which was almost always a hundred degrees, and then there was non-summer, when it was sixty degrees most days, but on the odd chance it got cold, let's say to forty-five degrees, we just pulled out the winter ski jackets and had a chance to make sure they still fit.

In Nashville this year we went from seventy degrees down to seventeen in a matter of forty-eight hours. Now, I love cold weather as much as anyone, but that seemed a bit abrupt.

My friend Shane was staying at my house for the week, sitting in my kitchen, when I came inside from running my dogs for the morning.

As I shed my multiple layers of coats and insulated pants, he looked at me and said: "This cold is horrible, let's go somewhere."

"Don't tempt me," I said.

Most of the country was below freezing. Chicago got to minus sixty-five degrees, and the airlines canceled hundreds of flights. There were not a lot of options.

"Let's go to Miami," I said. We had spent the previous evening video chatting with some friends in Miami, mostly being jealous of the weather and talking about that various ways we had come up with to pass the time when it was way too cold to go outside.

Shane is as dangerous and spontaneous as I am when it comes to rash last-minute decisions.

We both opened our laptops and started looking up flights, jokingly at first. It was dangerous from the get-go, and Shane was indulging me. Unfortunately, I could tell he was only half-committed. We both travel for a living, so we started checking our various air miles accounts, United MileagePlus for him and Delta SkyMiles for me.

We set a goal of arriving in Miami in time for dinner with our friends and started searching. Google Flights turned up a route that got us into Miami at 9 p.m. "That's a little late for dinner," I said.

"Nah, it's Miami, right on time," he shot back.

A few phone calls later, though, we were running into problems.

Apparently, we were not the only ones with the idea of "escape to the beach" during America's coldest day on record in decades.

I was starting to lose hope and, frankly, to get pretty frustrated. In my mind, we should already be sitting on South Beach sipping a drink at the Delano with our friends, deciding what we were going to order next.

I'm not sure what made Shane check Southwest, but I imagine the multiple ads we'd watched the night before during an NFL game might have had something to do with it.

We had some music playing in the background when he screamed out across the room, "HA! 'Wanna Get Away?' One-hundred-and-thirty-dollar one-way tickets. We can figure out how to get home some other day."

I was in shock. We hadn't seen a price of less than $1,000 during our search. "Only one problem," he said. "The flight leaves in an hour and a half."

I live a good forty-five minutes outside of Nashville, on a twenty-five-acre farm with five dogs. I can't just leave at a moment's notice without planning to have a farm sitter while I'm gone. That process usually takes me about a week, unless I get in a last-minute pinch and have to beg a friend of mine to come farm-sit for a few days.

"We will never make that flight," I said to Shane. "We are forty-five minutes away, and we haven't packed."

"There's nothing to pack, we are going to the beach, we need to leave in the next five minutes, LET'S GOOOOOOOO."

I sent a text message to my most reliable farm sitter and started throwing things in a backpack. I couldn't find my swimsuit, it was February. . . . I grabbed odds and ends out of my closet—a pair of jeans, shorts, a few T-shirts, a toothbrush—and we ran out the door.

Instead of incriminating myself, let's just say I drove a nice 75 mph on the forty-five-minute ride into Nashville. So we wouldn't have to check in at the counter and waste precious time, Shane was busy trying to log into both of our Southwest accounts to download our boarding passes, which turned out to be impossible because we were inside an hour of the scheduled departure.

I had the bright idea of valeting the car to save time, despite the price gouging. It's only forty-eight hours, right?

We ran into the Nashville International Airport and quickly scanned our credit cards at the Southwest kiosk, printed our boarding passes, and darted to security. It was starting to look like we had made it; the departure wasn't for twenty-five minutes. The security line at BNA comes in two flavors: deadlock, meaning it's gonna be an hour and a half, or entirely empty. We lucked into empty.

I was still jogging through the terminal once we cleared security, and Shane was already on the phone sauntering toward the gate. At one point I turned around looking for him and spotted him at the wine bar across from the entrance we were leaving from, ordering us two cold beers before we boarded.

As we sat sipping mimosas the next morning at the pool, he turned to me and just said: "Wanna get away?"

I don't want to promote foolish spending, reckless driving, or generally running out of your house at the last minute without a plan, but I have to say it was a blast. We both travel three hundred thousand miles a year, so it wasn't the first "throw shit in a bag and get out the door" experience for either of us, but it was the first time I had ever done it just for the sake of doing it, for fun. Keep an extra $500 lying around in your savings account if you can, for the next polar vortex. You never know when travel inspiration might strike.

Jeremy Jauncey

Jeremy is the founder and CEO of Beautiful Destinations, an award-winning creative agency that focuses on nation-branding, helping the leaders of countries and tourism boards understand the way the world sees them.

Jeremy is what you would call "Insta-famous." His personal profile has 702,000 followers, and Beautiful Destinations has 22 million followers across its various accounts, making it the largest tourism community in the world.

He grew up in Scotland and played rugby for the national team before turning his attention to travel, launching a business that has gained international recognition. Jeremy routinely speaks about travel as a force for good in the world, and he was the first person I thought of when I set out to write this book.

Daniel Houghton: I know you believe that travel can change the world. Why?
Jeremy Jauncey: It all starts from a very passionate belief that travel is a force for good—that it is this universal language to connect people all over the world. It's that unifying force that really does show that it doesn't matter the color of your skin, or how old you are, or where you come from, or your gender, or how much money you may or may not have.

The whole travel experience is so revolutionary. I was lucky to have had the chance to travel when I was young, but as Beautiful Destinations has developed as a business, I've been able to see firsthand the impact that travel can have on people as adults.

I tend to think about it in three different pillars. The first pillar is very personal. And it's the idea that if you travel in the world, and you go out there with an open mind, if you embrace new cultures, and meet new people, you can understand their perspectives. It's really as simple as going to a place and spending time in that culture.

The second pillar, which is equally as important, is the economic impact. We all know that travel is the second-biggest industry in the world; it's estimated that one in every ten jobs in the world is related to travel. It's a multitrillion-dollar industry that impacts the lives of millions and millions of people. When you go to a new country, and you invest your dollars into that country, you're having an immediate economic impact. I once heard someone say that travel is like the ATM of the world, because the moment that a tourist gets off the plane and lands in the country, they're spending dollars in that country. It's not like finance, or infrastructure, where you actually need time to develop things before you see a return.

The third, I think, is more situational. I think it's more related to the kind of world that we live in today—recognizing that there are leaders in government, in popular culture, in industry that are telling us we should be putting up walls, or sending people home, or judging people based on all of these different things, which, when you travel, you realize are in fact so insignificant: gender, age, race.

Travel has that kind of humanizing power, I believe, and I think this book is so timely right now, because social media and digital technologies allow us to share those travel experiences far, far wider than ever before.

You take a video of what it's like to land in an entirely new country, and share it with millions of people. It can genuinely change their perceptions about what that country is—no time or money required.

DH: Give me a little bit of an overview of some of the places you've been.
JJ: I've always made it my mission to experience as many different cultures as I can. I've experienced the Middle East, I've experienced Asia, I've experienced Australasia, Europe, the US. I think some of the most inspiring moments I've had were going, for example, to the Middle East for the very first time, having grown up with certain perceptions about the region, what that culture was like, what the people were like, and then having a firsthand experience that was the polar opposite of what I was expecting. It really, really opened my eyes for the first time.

Everyone's going to have different perspectives on different countries. But really, what was so empowering for me going to that region was that it was nothing like my preconception was. And on the flip side, when I went to Japan in my late twenties, it was the first time that I'd been to a country where I felt, actually, completely helpless.

I felt utterly alien there because I was the one that looked so dramatically different. I was the one that couldn't communicate, and I was the one that didn't know how to read the road signs, didn't know how to ask for a cab, didn't know how to put money onto my subway ticket.

That was such a humbling experience, and it opened my eyes to the power of travel all over again. I think when you're a kid, or when you're growing up, you always remember the tourists that come to your country as the strange ones, the foreigners, but until you go through that reverse experience, you don't have the appreciation for how exciting the world really is.

DH: When you think back on all those places, what's the one that you can't get out of your mind, that makes you go, "Wow, I can't believe I actually did that, and this is actually my life"?
JJ: I'd say maybe the most impactful journey that I've done recently would be a trip to Egypt about a month ago. Egypt's tourism industry took an extreme dive after the Arab Spring—although it's a country that is very, very heavily dependent on its tourism, and is steeped in culture and has probably influenced the childhood dreams of more people in the world than anywhere else.

When I went for the first time last month, I was very, very fortunate to be allowed to go into the Pyramids before the park was open, with a group of local guys who were horsemen. They took us out on horses and got us there at four thirty in the morning. We waited for an hour and a half for the sun to rise and had breakfast, just watching the sun rising over the Pyramids.

Having had those childhood experiences that I mentioned, reading about ancient Egyptian culture as a kid and seeing it in the books, imagining what it would be like to be there, that was probably one of the most surreal experiences I've ever had.

DH: Travel can be scary. That's hard for you and me to remember because we are on a plane every week, but there's a lot of people that haven't traveled anywhere. Talk to me about that, and what would you say to someone that's never been on an airplane?
JJ: The fear that you may feel about encountering new cultures, or feeling that somehow you would be alone when you travel, com-

pletely goes away when you realize that, inherently, you believe people are good, which I very passionately do, that that's true of people everywhere, regardless of their race, or their background, or the country that they come from.

The feeling around the world, stoked by the mainstream media, that we're all out to get each other, that we are all out to better ourselves, and when you encounter these people who maybe don't look quite the same as you or didn't have the same background as you did, they somehow look down on you, is just fundamentally wrong.

I think in my experience, there is a basic human understanding that we are good and that we will care about the same things— we all want to love and be loved. We want to build families and friendships, we want to be successful in whatever endeavor it is that we've undertaken.

That's the same whether you're Japanese, or from Senegal, or from London, or from Kentucky. And I don't think you can understand that until you genuinely experience it through travel.

The second thing I would say is that there is so much out in the world that we don't know. And there are so many unique things that happen when you travel, that the spontaneity of the experience is something that will absolutely, fundamentally change your life.

I think people who are afraid of travel or who don't want to travel have the understandable concern that change will make things worse. I have found in every single situation, even if, in the short term, I might have had a negative experience, the long-term effect of having gone through it is positive, and additive to my life.

I think the travel experience is one of those things that you can plan, you know, to the nth degree, how you want your travel experience to go, but there really is nothing like adapting to a change in plans, and experiencing something new.

One of the things I use as a tool to talk to people when I encounter those that haven't traveled, or are nervous about travel, is my phone. Just showing them on Instagram how amazing the world is—there's nothing that better illustrates the core of why our business has been successful.

We've been able to tap into this underlying desire of people, to want to have that moment of exhilaration, the kind of moment that takes them a thousand miles away. They may think it's unrealistic, but when you show them that beautiful sunset across a savannah in Zimbabwe, or the Shibuya Crossing in Tokyo, it just sparks that excitement for them.

I find that incredibly exciting, and I often see that when people have a look at those images or those videos that we're creating on Instagram, they kind of relax their guard a little bit and they think, "You know, maybe it would be fun to travel to that kind of place," or "Maybe I could see myself sitting on a beach or having a coffee in that city that I've never been to."

DH: Share a story of a trip that has gone ... spectacularly wrong.

JJ: On one particular occasion, I had to get back to New York City for a meeting, one that was incredibly commercially crucial to the business, and were I to miss it, the likelihood of us losing that account was very, very high.

New York City, whenever it gets snow, the whole place shuts down. You can see that if you're coming in from other airports. You begin to see all the flights getting locked down, then canceled.

So this time, my flight was canceled, and I got bumped onto

the next flight. They kept getting canceled. I think I got bumped five more times, onto different flights, none of which ever took off. Every time, I got my hopes up that I was going to make it.

Long story short, I didn't get back to New York in time for the meeting, but by complete happenstance, the client ended up having an emergency board meeting that day and had to cancel anyway.

I guess it was entirely serendipitous, because had we gone ahead with the meeting, the outcome would have been negative for us. Luckily, they had this board meeting come out of the blue, something changed, and we rescheduled the meeting to three weeks later. Turns out the changes that came from their emergency meeting made the outcome, instead, spectacularly positive for us. So we probably would have lost the business, but because of the turn of events we actually got an even bigger contract. Those are the things that make me really appreciate the travel experience, even though in the moment I was hating it.

DH: Sometimes all you need is a good snowstorm.
JJ: Exactly.

Captain Lee Rosbach

If you've turned on your TV in the last few years and found your-self binge-watching Bravo, I had you at "Captain Lee." Lee Ros-bach is the star of *Below Deck*, the reality show where he and his crew take wealthy guests on the experience of a lifetime aboard a megayacht. The show is in its seventh season and, eighty-five episodes in, doesn't show any signs of slowing.

I'm proud to admit I'm a huge fan of the show, and Lee in particular, so I reached out to him to see if we could get some travel inspiration from his unique and luxurious perspective.

Daniel Houghton: Captain Lee, it is great to meet you, sir.
Captain Lee: My pleasure.

DH: Where are you in the world right now? Are you filming or not? And then I'd love to hear how you got into the indus-try in the first place. Did you travel growing up?
CL: As far as traveling growing up, it never happened. I came from a broken family, so there weren't a lot of funds to go around. Going on vacation was the norm for a lot of people, but it wasn't for me, or at least up to that point. And the reason I've always wanted to travel—I just thought life was too short to stay in one place all that long, because there are just so many exotic and won-derful places in the world to see.

So many different cultures to experience. How you got there didn't really matter—the point was you got there, you had the experience. And sometimes just making the journey was the experience. So I just don't think there is a bad thing about traveling—packing, maybe, and unpacking.

DH: Yeah, that part can be rough. You can't really bring that much when you're living on a boat.
CL: The larger the boat, the more you can take with you. And believe me, the people that come on our boats bring a lot.

DH: They don't seem to be short on luggage!
CL: I think all they want are options. I would say they probably wear 10 percent of what they bring.

DH: Yeah.
CL: Which is probably also true in your own home.

DH: Lee, before you were a captain and when you first got into the industry, did you do an extensive amount of travel? Was that mostly kind of in and around North America? Or has it always been wherever the boat goes?
CL: My first real sojourn traveling was exploring a restaurant down in Turks and Caicos Islands. My family had restaurants in Indiana, in the northwest corner of Indiana, just outside of Chicago. So close to Chicago that we run the same time zone as Chicago, central time zone. And a friend of mine told me about a restaurant down in Turks and Caicos I might be able to buy. And I've always been one looking for adventure. I thought, "Why not?" So I went down there and took a look at it and we closed the deal on it.

I took the whole family down there. There was a series of circumstances that were beyond my control, and the hotel and casino that was going up two blocks from our restaurant never made it past the second floor. They ran out of money, couldn't get financing for it. So as a result, my long-term plans were fairly well shot. And to start a business on the island, you had to have a local partner.

DH: Sort of like starting a business in China ... interesting.
CL: So I had this island partner who was a ... questionable character, and I didn't know that for a very long time. I found out he had a serious drug problem that I had been supporting for a long time. And then after the cash was gone, I needed some work. Work permits were hard to come by, because it's very similar to Herman Wouk's *Don't Stop the Carnival.* If you're an islander, you get the first shot at any job. And only after they have exhausted all other possibilities would they give an expat a chance at it, so there is never full employment on the island.

DH: Right.
CL: So at any rate, there was a job as a deckhand on a sailboat going down to the British Virgin Islands, down to Sint Maarten. And I needed the money. So I took the job. And that was my first venture, traveling by water. When I came back, I told my wife, "I love it. That's what I want to do. I want to be a captain, I want to be on boats."

DH: How many years before you were captaining your first boat?
CL: Probably five years. And that was working really, really diligently. First you had to get back to the States, then we had to regroup, replenish the bank account a little bit, and move to where the boats were, which was Florida. And then we had to get jobs when we first moved to Florida. I would work part-time on boats, work for nothing, just so I could get sea time so I could sit for my

exam. After I got my license, I would captain anything that floated. I didn't care. Just to get enough sea time to increase my license.

DH: Lee, I think a lot of people that watch the show have probably been somewhere in the Caribbean. Last season, you all went on a little bit of an international adventure. I like to think that you all are semi-responsible for showing people the world. And although they may not experience it on a superyacht, I hope that encourages them to get out there however they can.

I know you probably don't have a lot of time off the boat in those places, but I'd love to hear just a little bit about your observations. It must be amazing to show people those things for the first time.

CL: That part of it never gets old. There are certain parts of every destination that I've traveled that I think are just jaw-dropping. If you go to the British Virgin Islands and you go to the end of Virgin Gorda, and you look at the baths and you look at the size of those boulders, and you just go, "How in the world did these things ever get here?"

DH: It's crazy. My parents took me for the first time when I was eleven. And I was like, "What is this alien planet that we're on?"
CL: You really get a kick out of sharing it with people because on the way there you can build the anticipation. And you say, "You're really not going to believe this. You're just not ready for what I'm going to show you." And then you get there and look at the expression on their faces—it makes it all worthwhile.

DH: I know you've had crew members from all over the world. I'd like to think you've had the opportunity to shape a lot of

those young people's lives. Talk to me a little bit about those relationships.

CL: I think a lot of times with the kids, when they first get into the yacht, they don't fully comprehend the enormity of the world that's out there. I think the best way to experience the world is by boat, because it gives you access to so many different places and things that are usually inaccessible.

DH: Yeah, I have to agree with you there.

CL: You see things that, hell, only a handful of people in the world have ever seen. Because let's face it, there are only five thousand megayachts in the world. And most stay tied up at the dock.

I try to impart to these kids how lucky they are to be getting paid to do this. To go places that most people only dream about. I mean, having lunch at a waterfall in Tahiti . . . how many people that you know can actually say they have done that?

DH: Probably very, very few.

CL: Appreciate it and don't take it for granted, you know? Don't act like the millennial you are.

DH: Correct. I hate that stereotype. Unfortunately, most of the time it's true. But you probably got to witness a lot of growth and maturity over the years, especially with people that you've worked with. I know you've watched people become true professionals that probably were still struggling to tie a knot when they first stepped on your boat.

CL: It's fun to watch people morph into something they never thought they could be. And just because they stuck with it—with a little encouragement, and a little education. They really pro-gressed as people.

DH: Absolutely. I think travel hits the fast-forward button on that.

CL: It sure does. You learn that there is a lot more to this world than the United States. There are a lot of different cultures, and some of them you're going to like; some of them, not so much. But, you still have to respect the people that live there. That's theirs. And when you're there, you have to adapt.

DH: Right, you're on their turf. And it's I think up to each of us to do our homework and understand the culture. Not that you have to take a college course on it before you visit. But it's fun to be informed. And it helps you make friends.

CL: Sure. Understand what good manners are in that particular part of the world. You may do something that you consider funny back home, but it is offensive somewhere else. So you need to take the time to research how you're going to get along in this new place.

DH: Lee, when you all are positioning and before guests ar-rive, in the downtime when you don't have guests on board, do you get off the boat and get to spend some time in some of these places and countries? Do you go up and just relax and have a beer and a nice meal, or are you a sightseer?

CL: I try to be as impulsive as I can. I like to go down to where the restaurants aren't quite so nice and where the street vendors sell their things. If I'm in a Latin American country, I might go down to the barrio. I find myself a little cantina, hang out, and get some really authentic food, because that's where I find out most about the culture. You know, five-star treatment is five-star treatment anywhere in the world. The sheets are a certain thread count. The hotel has made sure everything is done for you. All the *t*'s are crossed, all the *i*'s are dotted, and that's not really how you find out about a country or a way of life. I think you find out by getting out and experiencing some of the things that are not so pretty.

DH: I've been asking everyone about something that went wrong on a trip that they can laugh about now. Is there any particular story that jumps out at you? It doesn't have to be from the show.
CL: I can think of one funny thing. My wife and I flew down to Haiti on an old twin-engine Beechcraft. It could hold six people—seven if someone didn't mind sitting on a cooler of beer between the pilot and copilot. When we got there, the whole country was on strike. We landed at the airport and then we couldn't buy fuel because they wouldn't pump it, so we had to bribe somebody to go siphon fuel out of another airplane. We wanted to see the Citadelle.

DH: Oh wow, that must have been amazing.
CL: It was amazing. It was quite a trip just to get there. You'd go halfway up the mountain by four-wheel drive, and the other half you went by horseback with some little kid pulling the horse up the mountainside—walking behind him, hanging on to his tail, hitting him with a switch to get him to keep going. The amount of poverty that was there—and that was thirty years ago—was incredible, and it was rather depressing. But I was so glad we went.

DH: I think it's important to travel to places like that. Because you then come home and everything's comfortable, and

you see a story on the news, and at least you have some sense of it. And it can create empathy.

Lee, if you could wave a magic wand and say, "This is where I would like to run my next charter," where would that be?

CL: Right now it would probably be the Galápagos.

DH: Are there a lot of superyachts that go down there, or are they more privately owned?

CL: Private. Yeah, I mean it's so expensive. The government down there, they charge you. If you bring your own boat, they charge you two hundred and fifty dollars per person, per day. Including crew. On a megayacht, we might have twelve guests and thirteen crew.

DH: It's a multi-thousand-dollar day, and you haven't even run the engines yet.

CL: I guess it's a way to keep people away—to keep it unspoiled. But if money were no object, yeah, I could see myself spending a month there.

DH: Amazing. Yeah, that would be a lot of fun. I have never been there. It's high on the list for me as well.

CL: Yeah. I just try to stay away from the normal places that people find you—the French Riviera, for example. That doesn't impress me a lot. I'm not a big fan of the Mediterranean either. It's hard to experience, because it seems like everyone over there has a see-and-be-seen attitude. It's like, "Look at me, I've arrived."

DH: Where do you travel with your wife these days?

CL: This year we are going to go to Charleston. We've been up there once before. I like the city. It's got a lot of great restaurants, great culture, and I love taking the buggy tour around the city with someone who actually knows their history. They can tell you that the ceiling on the porch is painted a particular color because back in the 1600s, they believed it would ward off warlocks.

DH: I just bought a house, and I painted the porch ceilings that color. I have a theory that it actually keeps bugs away, but maybe I'm crazy. It sure looks nice.

CL: Yeah, and I love the architecture in Charleston. It's such a genteel city.

DH: I have one last question, Lee. When you look back at all the places you've been, how do you think travel has changed you as a person? Has it opened your mind? Has it made you a lot of new friends?

CL: I think what it does is remind me of how truly fortunate I am to be able to do what I do, get paid for it, and just be comfortable. I'm so grateful for that. There are a lot of people out there that don't ever get to do a fraction of what I have. So I don't feel guilty about it, but I do feel very lucky. And it kind of keeps things in perspective.

DH: Okay, actual last question. When you think ten, fifteen, twenty years from now, what comes to mind? Are you going to continue as a captain? Or do you have an end date in mind?

CL: I try to knock off one or two places on my bucket list a year. Retirement, I don't know if that's a really good thing. I'm not a huge fan of retirement.

CHAPTER 6

HOW TO EMBRACE THE SPIRIT OF ADVENTURE

One of the most common reasons people cite for traveling is adventure.

It's a word that every person I've interviewed for this book has mentioned at least once. And with good reason—it's human nature to seek the new, but also to fear it a little.

Travel is a series of both knowns and unknowns. You can start a journey knowing where you're going, what flight you're taking to get there, and hopefully an idea of where you're going to stay, what language the locals speak, and how to move about town.

The unknowns are much more, and you don't have to wait until you get to where you're going to let the adventure begin. Airports can be fascinating places. I've spent time in probably seventy-five to a hundred airports around the world, and they range from the mundane to the absolutely mind-boggling.

The first time I stepped off an Emirates plane in Dubai, I discovered that there were multiple stories, for the various flight classes—a floor for first class, another for business, and another for . . . everyone else. They all have identical shops, but you don't have to mix with your fellow travelers until you're all stuck on the same plane.

I once checked into an airline lounge in Sydney only to discover that there was a spa on-site. "A spa?" I asked. "Yes, sir, would you like to make an appointment?"

I would, and I did. I had never been to a spa at that point in my life, but I booked a half-hour massage in the most stunning space I've ever seen at an airport, overlooking the runway as planes took off and landed.

Adventure at the airport can also mean less than exciting accommodations. I've never had it quite as bad as Tom Hanks in the terminal, but I have dragged chairs together, thrown blankets over my suitcase, and made temporary housing to survive a day-long weather delay when I couldn't keep my eyes open anymore.

When I asked Lonely Planet editorial director Tom Hall what travel meant to him, adventure was top of mind.

"I think that the word *travel* is really a gateway to other words. The next word that comes to mind is *discovery*, and the one after that is an *adventure*. Adventure has an instantly uplifting effect. Part of it is in the memories of what I have been lucky enough to do, and part of it is what I hope to do in the future."

You really never do know quite what you're getting into when you start a trip. Sometimes you wind up in a set of circumstances you could never have imagined.

On one such trip I was in Australia for work and was supposed to be spending the weekend in Sydney, when a meeting got moved, and I realized I was going to need to be in Melbourne first thing Monday morning instead. Instead of being able to fly out on the first flight Monday, I needed to head to the airport and spend the weekend in Melbourne instead.

When I got there, I had no plans other than catching up on some sleep from the jet lag. I wound up having lunch at a place a ton of locals had recommended, and I only managed to get a seat because the hostess helped me find a place at the bar that was supposed to be taken but someone had missed their reservation.

We ended up talking for a bit before I left, and I walked out the door with an invite to hang out with a group of friends later that day over a few beers. I didn't have any friends in town and really just knew people from work, so the idea of spending some time with some people my age in a city I didn't know much about sounded fun.

I met up with them a few hours later, and we proceeded to descend into an unplanned pub crawl all over town. We kept meeting more friends and running into people that knew each other and gaining members of the tour as we went along.

Several hours and several bars later we went down a very narrow street to a place that looked like it didn't have much seating. It was the kind of place you would never find unless someone walked you right up to it.

When I went up to the bar to order, the bartender started talking to me, and he eventually came around from behind the bar to join us for a drink and conversation. It turns out, it was his bar, he was the owner. He started telling me how he was working on the roof so they could expand and walking me through the design and the whole story of how he wound up starting the joint in the first place.

A few drinks in, he invited me to a post near the corner of the bar where he had begun to mark the heights of various patrons he had befriended since the place opened. I'm six-four, which is pretty tall, but a long way from being really tall in America. After he measured and I stepped away I realized I had claimed the prize, tallest person to date. I didn't pay for a drink for the rest of the evening. He and I are still friends to this day, and although we haven't seen each other in person since that evening, we message back and forth. I wouldn't dare set foot in Australia without calling him first.

Kevan Chandler

Kevan Chandler is one of the most inspiring travelers you could ever hope to meet. Born with a neurological disease that prevents him from walking, he has lived his entire life in a wheelchair. Realizing that his desire to travel wasn't going away, he enlisted the help of several friends and fashioned a backpack that he could be carried around in. They all flew to Europe, and his friends took turns carrying him around Paris, getting lost just like the rest of us. He shared his incredible perspective with me.

Kevan Chandler: Good morning, sir. How you doing?

Daniel Houghton: Good. Thanks for making the time. I would love to hear just a little bit about who you are and what you do, before we launch into the travel stuff.

KC: Sure. I'm thirty-two years old. I was born in South Florida and grew up in the middle of North Carolina, and now I'm in northern Indiana. When I was about a year and a half or two years old, I was diagnosed with spinal muscular atrophy, which is a neuromuscular disease that comes in waves on the motherboard of your brain and just kind of messes up the message to the limbs, causing the muscles to atrophy.

So I've spent most of my life in a wheelchair; I was never really able to walk. I have an older sister who's also diagnosed with MA, and she was able to walk till she was five or six. And my older brother is perfectly fine. So my parents just decided to raise me and my sister as normally as possible from day one. Of course, that required some extra effort for some things. But for the most part, we went to church with our friends, we went to a normal public school, and I played soccer with kids and, you know, just lived a pretty normal life.

We also had kind of an open-door policy, where not only were we out in the world, but always had people staying with us, hanging out. So it really normalized disabilities to the world around us. When people saw my sister and me, they jumped in and helped because it was just what you did. It also helped me to kind of normalize being disabled in an able-bodied world. So I've never really had huge expectations of what the world needs to be for me, because I invite people to help me and I just kind of figure things out and create a community around me, where I pour into them as much as they pour into me.

What that has fostered is a whole slew of rich and profound friendships which I'm really, really blessed to have. I was actually reading a book a few months ago called the *Bond of Brotherhood*, and it's about the struggle that men have in communicating their deeper feelings, and teaching one another beyond just talking about sports or the weather or stuff like that. And I'm reading it, thinking, "It sounds like he's absolutely right in that most men have like one or two, if they're lucky, guys that they can really connect with on a deeper level. I've got like thirty in my life. This is awesome."

So I'm just really blessed to have that, and I think it comes from my personal needs, including physical needs, and also my desire to engage others for their needs as well. So that's kind of a world that I grew up in. My dad was an airplane mechanic with Piedmont, and then US Air. So, not only did we get flights everywhere, but because he was from the west coast of Canada and my mom was from Florida, we have family everywhere. It was a lot of time, a lot of road trips—boys on the move. Luckily, my dad being a mechanic—as you probably know with your dad—he can pretty much fix or build anything.

DH: Literally anything. Yeah.
KC: It's like, when you start with airplanes, you're pretty much just working backwards.

DH: Everything else is easier. They can do plumbing, electricity.
KC: Exactly.

DH: He's not that great with woodworking, although I've picked that up. But he can pretty much fix anything—air conditioners, HVACs, whatever. He replumbed my entire first house in a weekend!
KC: Yeah, so growing up with that, and just the spirit of let's take a step back. Look at what we have and work with it. And my mom was the same way. She was a pro-life advocate through the eighties and nineties, really on the front lines. So that's kind of a world I grew up in. Getting up every day, seeing what I can do, and seeing what I want to do and kind of finding the balance in between. Getting creative like that. When I got into high school, I played in bands. We definitely traveled a lot—high school and college.

DH: What instrument did you play?
KC: I played harmonica and sang. And yeah, so then got into college and moved out in the dorms with some friends. And I figured I was already traveling with my friends there, maybe they can take care of me in a living situation. So I did that, like

half an hour from home. And then I moved nine hours away after school—moved up here in Fort Wayne, and I've been here for about five years. And in between there I moved to Arkansas to work in prison ministry for a while. Then went back to North Carolina. But yeah, I had always wanted to go to Europe. Just because of my family's heritage, and also to see the art and music. I love the early-twentieth-century British authors, like Chesterton, J. M. Barrie, and Tolkien, of course. So I wanted to go and be where all of that happened. I wrote about Reinhardt, who was a gypsy that wandered around France playing guitar during World War II. So yeah, I always wanted to do this stuff and always figured, well, it's probably impossible because so many of the things I want to do there aren't wheelchair accessible.

DH: Especially a lot of the old historic . . . well, Europe as a whole can be difficult for wheelchairs. Talk to me about going abroad for the first time.
KC: So that was in 2016. Two years before, I was in North Carolina hanging out with some friends and we decided to go urban spelunking in the sewers of Greensboro. So we kind of came up with this makeshift backpack using a metal frame.

DH: Did you just say to them, "Hey, I want to go with you, let's figure out if we can make this work"?
KC: Actually, it was the other way around. One of my friends was like, "Hey, I've always wanted to check out the sewers. Do you want to come?" I was like, "Sure. Why not?" And we had talked about doing something outside of my chair, just because, you know, we're used to that. For example, we go to a friend's

house and there are steps, right, we just leave my chair outside. We were like, "What if we did something a little more without the chair?" So we put this weird makeshift backpack together and went down for, like, three hours into the sewers. It worked so well that that summer, I was like, "You know what, I've always wanted to go to Europe. The stuff I want to do is in the countryside and not accessible. But apparently, now we can do that!"

DH: Right, "We figured this out with the backpack!"
KC: Right. I've always kind of lived in that mindset, but not to this extent, of course. And so I emailed that same guy, and was like, "Hey, what if we do that again, except in Europe for three weeks and aboveground?" And he was all for it. And so we got four guys, we started a GoFundMe, and a year later, exactly a year later, from that day, we were in Paris. And that's the short version.

DH: Wow. Now, do you routinely fly on airplanes? That part wasn't unusual for you? It was just "I'm going to Europe for the first time."
KC: Right. So I had only flown around the North American continent. But I mean, we left my wheelchair at the airport. Yeah, so that was the big thing—when we leave this hotel on Sunday morning and get on the bus to go to the airport, it's backpack or nothing for three weeks.

DH: Right.
KC: And we had four guys carry me. That was the big difference between my other flying experiences. We got to the Atlanta airport six hours early, because we had no idea what they were going to do when we walked up with me in a backpack, right?

DH: What happened?

KC: It only took, like, ten minutes. It was crazy. They didn't even take me out of the backpack. They just took me off the guy's back and had him walk through. And they gave me a pat-down and they're like, all right, you're good to go. It's like the easiest experience ever.

DH: And then what happened when you went through customs when you landed in Paris? Like, same situation? You just went up there together and that was it?

KC: It actually wasn't a big deal on that end. Because sitting on the airplane, I was not in the backpack. Just, you know, on my own. So getting off the airplane, they just put me in a manual chair. So it was just like anybody else.

DH: Nice. So that wasn't a big deal. How was traveling through Europe, and all the things that come with that? How is that different than you going around North America?

KC: I mean, I loved the public transportation. The metro and the train and all of that, we really utilized that. We didn't rent a car or anything. So that was really great. The only tricky thing was that there were seven of us.

DH: That's a lot of people to keep up with, traveling as a group.

KC: Yeah, but we needed that many to make this happen, since we had four guys rotating through the lifting, and two guys filming the whole experience. So yeah, there were some complications in keeping everybody together and having them trade off carrying me and finding the right timing for that. But if you think about it, we didn't have to be worried about whether there were stairs, or, you know, if a train or a metro was actually accessible.

We just jumped on, and that was really awesome. This past October I was back in England and Ireland, with my wheelchair, and it was just interesting to see the difference. You have to call ahead to make sure they have ramps ready to get you off the Tube. It was fine, but it was different. The same principle holds with or without the chair: as long as I have friends around and we're willing to be flexible and creative, then it's going to go right in the end.

DH: It's inspiring to hear you say that, considering how much anxiety even able-bodied people have around travel and transport, especially flying. It sounds like it was basically just a mindset that you had—and that you've had your whole life—that, my disability isn't going to stop me, I'll figure this stuff out as I go?

KC: Yeah, it definitely was. And also, it could never have happened without the mindset of the other guys. The only things that I can do are dream, cast a vision, and be inspiring to other people, but these guys brought it home. So it was all them as well. We kind of have a running joke that people are like, "Oh, you're so brave for doing all this." And I'm like, "You guys are the ones that actually have to do it."

DH: Talk to me a little bit about how travel has changed you as a person. You've lived a pretty dynamic life so far. What has international travel made you realize about yourself, or the world?

KC: Well, um, I, before I answer that, I do want to add that this past year we kind of did our follow-up trip. But back in September, we went to China. With a group called Show Hope. Do you know Phil Shay?

DH: I don't. I haven't met Phil personally, but I used to work in the same building as Show Hope.

KC: Nice. Yeah. He's awesome and he also seems to know everybody, so I wanted to ask. So anyway, we went with Show Hope. It was cool because the first trip the focus was like "Hey, this is an adventure that we want to have just as a bunch of guys doing, you know, dumb stuff for ourselves." Whereas on this trip we went to spend time with the kids and the staff at their care centers and just be an encouragement to them. So it was a lot more mission-based.

DH: It was a different purpose.

KC: Right. We did that to kind of take the focus off of ourselves. And so to answer your question, how has travel changed me, I would say it's done a lot of things. One thing is that, and you've probably heard this from all your people, which is that I look at the world and I see it as reachable—not in an arrogant way. But it's like, I've been to Ireland, I've been to China. If I wanted to go somewhere, I mean, I may not be able to do it today or tomorrow, but eventually I'll make it work and go—it is possible.

DH: Right.

KC: I talked to someone the other day, and they were like, "So, everyone asks, what's your next big trip?" And I kind of give a rote answer for that. But I realized that while there are historical sites and, you know, natural wonders that I would like to experience, there's nowhere that I'm really dying to go. It's more that there are people that I want to be with. People I want to spend time with that are spread out everywhere. People that I met in different places, and people that I grew up with that have moved. I think traveling also helps sharpen your priorities.

DH: Tell me about that.
KC: I want to be careful how I say this. I can have crazy adventures and I can do crazy stuff with my friends. But at the same time, I think traveling has kind of gotten that bug out of me, as far as needing it, being a thrill seeker. It's given me like a contentedness to enjoy the people that are most dear to me. I think traveling and seeing the world makes you realize that every person you pass, everyone sitting on the train, has a full life of their own that you don't know anything about. They have things on their mind, and relationships of their own. And I think it kind of reminds you of the preciousness of your own relationships.

DH: I completely agree. And actually, no one has said that to me yet, but I have often felt the same way when I get home. It makes you really appreciate not just everything that you have, but the people in your life. To be honest, it makes me feel very content.
KC: Yeah, definitely. And then the guys that I travel with—I know some people like to travel alone, but it really gives you a shared experience that no one else can share with you. I mean, we get together now, and whether we talk about it or not, we have this kind of brotherhood. So travel does create these interesting dynamics in your relationships with people.

DH: I totally agree. I've been asking this question to everyone, and the answers have been lighthearted, hilarious, cringe-

worthy, all of the above. Tell me a story about one of your travels where something just went horribly wrong.

KC: Oh, which one do you want? So when we were in Europe, we were actually lost constantly. We would think we knew what we were doing, and then it wouldn't happen that way. So there was the day that we were leaving Paris, we decided to take the Chunnel from Paris to London. We had bought the tickets. And we even asked a police officer the night before—we showed him the tickets and said, you know, "Is this right? Is this where we're going?" So we thought we had everything figured out.

We got up the next morning and we had time to spare and we already were packed—everything was looking good. And we get to the train station and one of the guys looks at the tickets and looks up at the board and goes, "Guys, we're at the wrong station." We only had like thirty minutes, so we booked it all the way across the city. It's just like jumping from one metro to another, just trying to figure out where we're going, what we're doing. We lost one of the guys because his ticket wouldn't work at the gate in the metro—the scanner was a dud. And then one of our cameramen got on a car before we could and the doors closed. It was one thing after another, but we got to the right station and up to the gate. And the guy was like, "No, you're too late. We've already closed the gate." Because this was also the week that they announced Brexit. And so they were redoing all the security.

So we're standing there going, "These were pretty expensive tickets. What do we do?" Me and two other guys went into the ticket office and we talked to the guy, and usually they don't do refunds, you would just have to buy tickets for the next train. But we went in to the guy, we gave him the spiel that like, "You know, we went to the wrong station, is there any way you can help us," and he looked at the guys, and he looked at me, and he picks up the phone and has a conversation in French with his superior. And then he hangs up and he goes, "I'm just going to change your tickets to the next train," and we're like, "Aw, man, that's good." So we did get on the train. But it was definitely like in all the movies when you're late for your flight or your train, running through the station. It was invigorating. And the guys ran with me on their back. Which was new for me—I've never run in my entire life.

DH: That's awesome. Hey, what ended up happening with the video you took?
KC: We made a thirty-minute documentary. And we've actually just submitted it to Amazon. It should be up in the next few days.

DH: Okay, great. Tell me the name so people can search for it on Amazon.
KC: Sure. It's called *The View from Here*. Okay. And yeah, it should be on Amazon by the time the book comes out.

DH: That's awesome. And were you the executive producer? Or do you feel like you were directing it and shaping the creative vision of it? Or were you just the subject?
KC: I was a producer, I was definitely involved. But the guy that made it, the guy that filmed, directed, and edited the whole film was a friend of mine from North Carolina. And we have worked on other projects together. So when we decided to do the trip, he was one of the first people I called. I was like, "Dude, if we're gonna do this, we need to prove that we did it. I trust you and your vision." So when we got home, he kind of sorted through all

the footage—I think it was nine terabytes of footage—and while we did that, I wrote the first draft of the memoir. So I gave him that draft. And he essentially went through with a highlighter and marked the parts that he wanted to use for the documentary, found the relevant footage, and crafted the thirty-minute film from that. So all the narration is from the book; it kind of functions as a companion piece.

Readers: The book is called *We Carry Kevan: Six Friends. Three Countries. No Wheelchair.*

DH: Nice. That's awesome. Thank you so much for making the time to chat with me. Is there anything else you want to add? And I'll send you a recording of all this.
KC: Cool, yeah. Thanks, man. The only other thing I think I'd add from the disability standpoint of it is, as I've traveled and spoken with people, they're like, "How can you do this with your disability?" I meet different people with different disabilities, and they have dreams of traveling too. My thought process is always, like you said, baby steps. When it's warm, I can walk into town by myself, which is about a two-mile trek. So my mindset is, well, if I can manage that by myself . . .

DH: It's a long way! Most people would not walk two miles.
KC: Right, right. And it's like, so if I can do that with my disability, well, what's another, you know, X hundred miles on an airplane with my friends? It's all a ratio, it's all exponential. If you can do this little thing, well, then, maybe you can do this bigger thing. And so when people with disabilities ask me, if you have

supplements or medical gear, or exercises that you have to do, how do you transfer all that to traveling? But the thing is, you're still living your life. You just kind of take it with you. And I really believe it's important for everyone to experience new places. It even kind of puts your needs into perspective, and I'm really grateful that because of my traveling, I figured out what I need and what I don't, and what I thought I needed because of my disability and what I don't. And I think your expectations of comfort change, and what you think you need changes.

I mean, for example, this morning, I packed my suitcase for a trip this week. And it's like, I threw basically all my clothes in, not because I needed a lot of clothes, but because I don't have a lot. So my travel life looks just like my everyday life now. And I think that happens with medical stuff too. You kind of realize that "If I'm traveling, I don't need this machine." Or "I don't need this aspect of my wheelchair." Or "I don't need a special bed. I can sleep on a couch for a few nights." And then you come and go. I did all right with that.

DH: Yeah, it's just part of adapting.
KC: Yeah, exactly. Tiny travel was great for that too.

DH: That's awesome. It's the same thing we all have to go through. Most people just end up schlepping a whole bunch of stuff all over the planet. And then you realize when you're there and don't touch half of what you brought.
KC: Right. Exactly. I mean, it's definitely scary at first. I've been really blessed to not need a lot of medical stuff. But I did leave my wheelchair home, you know, for three weeks.

DH: Yeah, your main mode of transport.

KC: It made me realize so much more fully that while it is useful, it's not absolutely necessary. And it made me trust the people around me more. That just enriched so many relationships.

DH: That's awesome. Kevin, thank you so much. I loved getting to know you. Please look me up when you come down.

KC: Definitely, man. Thanks.

Anisa Kamadoli Costa

Anisa Kamadoli Costa is a sustainability executive, philanthropy expert, and coalition builder. She is the chairman and president of The Tiffany & Company Foundation, as well as chief sustainability officer at Tiffany & Company—two distinct, yet synergistic roles that embody Tiffany's long-standing commitment to environmental and social responsibility. As CSO, Anisa directs Tiffany's global sustainability agenda, improving global corporate standards, minimizing the company's environmental impact, and driving partnerships across the for-profit and nonprofit sectors. In her role at the foundation, she oversees strategic grant-making focused on responsible mining and coral conservation.

Daniel Houghton: Anisa, thank you so much for making the time. Give me your travel history right out of the gate!
Anisa Kamadoli Costa: I'll start off by saying that travel is something that I feel has always been instilled in me by my parents. My parents came over from India, to New York. My father actually got a scholarship to graduate school at Cornell—this was so long ago that he actually came over on a ship. When he was a kid growing up under British rule in India, he actually loved the British. He also loved what he had learned about America. So he just applied to grad school, got in, and then met my mother over here.

I mention the part about my parents coming over because, at a time when travel was much less frequent, they always talked about the different countries they had visited. So I grew up very mindful of the world being so much bigger than New York, or the United States.

We traveled to almost every state in the US during my childhood, because of my father's job. So even that for me was an amazing experience, because I'm such a globalist by nature; when it comes to trying to decide where to go for vacation, I usually tend to leave the US. But by the same token, there just simply is not enough time, because whenever I do go to Montana, or Utah, or places that are not your typical business travel destinations, I remember how lucky we are, because the world, including America, just has so many amazing, really special places that have such beauty.

So growing up, I saw a lot of America, but I also got to travel internationally, especially back to India. I went to boarding school, and we did a trip, one of the more memorable ones I've taken, to Spain. That was probably my first trip, sort of on my own with friends, and it gave me this sense of adventure and excitement about learning other cultures.

DH: Talk to me about your career, and how travel injected itself. It seems like it almost took over, to guide your path in life.

AKC: Yes, it's always guided what I was interested in. I worked with the US mission to the United Nations.

I realized that getting to know local cultures and communities was something that was important to me. I'd say that was driven by my time at the UN, but was able to manifest itself when I was at the Rockefeller Brothers Fund, which is a private family foundation for the Rockefeller family. There are a lot of people that travel for work, and that's great. But one of the things that I've always been very appreciative of is that my job has taken me places where I'm not just siting in a windowless conference room working on spreadsheets, but out there working proactively on social and environmental issues with a global group of people.

Then that brought me to Tiffany & Company, because I met the then-chairman and CEO, who had just established the Tiffany & Company Foundation. They had the legal framework, and wanted someone with philanthropic expertise to come and help build the foundation from the ground up. That led to a whole host of other things, including working with Richard Branson on some of his initiatives, among lots of other amazing experiences.

DH: What was it like to start that at a company like Tiffany's, a company known to have the highest retail sales per square foot of any company in the world outside of Apple? How did you get that off the ground in such an established business?
AKC: It's a pretty humbling experience, and you definitely feel sort of a weight to it in a good way, right? Because it's Tiffany, it's a globally recognized and respected brand. And there are very few brands that people trust so much.

It has been a real privilege working with the board and the CEO, and the senior team overall, to develop this long-term philanthropic strategy, and then actually growing our CSR efforts into a true global sustainability program. And now we're at the point where we're looking at and talking about what it means to be a purpose-driven company.

To be able to work at an American company that's more than 182 years old, that is really significant. Anything we do, anywhere that we invest, philosophically or as a company, there's a lot that comes to bear. We try to use our voice and brand in ways that are responsible, and to advance agendas that we are supportive of.

And it's nice that we're so distinctively American, an American luxury brand. There are very few of those. But we're so global that when you go to our store in Milan, yes, it feels like a Tiffany store. But it also feels like it's a local store. We're working to balance the global with the local. And I think that's really critical.

DH: I'm an optimist, so I like to think that most companies, especially large global companies, want to do the right thing, and either have some sort of CSR initiative in place, or know that they should and are working toward it. What advice would you give to people in power at other companies, or someone in a role like yours at another business?

AKC: I would recommend the power of collaboration. And that, again, ties back to travel, because you can collaborate no matter what sector or issue the person or organization is passionate about. In fact, you need to collaborate to effect the change in a timely fashion, whether it's climate, diversity, or any other issue.

Now more than ever, I think businesses in this sector have a larger role to play. And now people understand the power that business has to be a positive social change. And therefore, I think there's that much more responsibility.

To understand that we're living in a very interconnected world, that we can't think about things in silos, we can't think about the environment in one silo, and people in another silo. And similarly, we can't think about business in one silo and government in another. Everyone has a role to play, frankly, in every major issue we confront as a society. And I think if we don't experience "the other," then we won't realize that there isn't really an "other," but only a bunch of people that all need to fit together.

DH: Amen.

AKC: I can't remember if it was a specific question that you sent in advance, but I was thinking about the evolution of my style of travel over the years, and when I was younger, it was very much sort of traveling without even thinking about it, right?

Now, one of the things that I started to realize that I was missing when traveling for work is the little things, like taking public transportation. Not just because it's good for the environment, but because that's where you meet and talk to people, either locals or other travelers. I think people accidentally segment themselves off without realizing it, so I've been working to change things up more often.

If I'm traveling with our family or even alone, I like to change up the hotel, instead of just always staying where I do for work. I used to always just go back to the same hotel, but I'm trying to be more and more thoughtful and pointed about those decisions.

DH: I absolutely know what you mean. I used to spend two-thirds of my year on the road, most of the time only for a day or two at a time in each location. It's easy to forget what you're doing and zone out when you're just there for a business meeting and then flying right out. It's important to make the time to wander around and experience a place, even if you've been there a hundred times before.

AKC: I recently heard someone speak at a conference I was at, and he was saying that the best way to create memories, really long-lasting memories, was just to see where things take you. Go for a walk and get lost!

DH: All right, switching gears a little bit, I don't know how much time you get to spend mentoring or talking to young people, but what would you say to someone if they looked at you and said, "All this travel stuff is great, but I'm pretty happy where I'm at and I don't know why you keep going on about it!"

AKC: For someone who hasn't necessarily felt the desire to leave their home country or home, I'd imagine one of the reasons is that the US is a pretty rich experience, right? And that's absolutely correct. But imagine how much richer your experience could be when you start to experience that at a global level, country by country and region by region. I think that sometimes, especially as Americans, we tend to sort of bring things here. Like, we will call something Indian food. And yes, of course it's Indian food, but within India, or China, there are so many specialties and regional components that are so amazing that you are missing out on!

So having a chance to meet the people, and see the beauty of the places and spaces. Historical architecture, or just the natural beauty that we find in different countries. I think sometimes we take it for granted. I feel very lucky that I've had the ability to go to the Arctic Circle, and to Bristol Bay, Alaska. I mean, each place is so breathtaking in its own way. And when you see how the local culture has evolved, because of the geography, and climate, and you know, how that connects to cultural celebrations and how that connects to food, and what drives tourism, it's pretty spectacular. I'm just constantly worrying that I'm never going to make it to all the places that I want to visit.

DH: I need to go!

AKC: Right! Exactly. Then add in all the places that I want to go back to, again, or take my kids to. I'm always looking at the calendar to see, what can we squeeze in? Where and with whom, right, because there's such value in traveling alone, but also with family, and how you figure out ways to combine that, whether it's meeting up with friends in their home country or meeting up with someone else's family in the place you're going. I just, I think when you mix in the people and relationships, travel becomes very special.

DH: It's always amazing when you get to spend real time with people who actually live in other countries, following them around. It's one thing to get an Airbnb and play house, but it's another thing to spend time with your friends in other countries and do normal things, like go to the grocery store, pick up their kids from school, and run the errands.

Tell me your favorite story of traveling with your kids. What sticks out the most? And I don't care if the answer is Disney World because they cried tears of joy. What is the most special trip for you and the family?

AKC: When they were four and five years old, we adopted our children from India, and because the adoption process is so long, we spent a long time in a hotel in India. So it was a little like Eloise. There's the pool and the buffet, and they were four and five—they loved it! And still to this day, when we go back, every other year, I ask, "Hey, what's your favorite part?" And they say the buffet and the pool. I say this jokingly, to you, because that's sort of the exact opposite of everything I just told you in terms of what you should care about when you travel somewhere.

DH: Well, from your children's perspective, it sounds like maybe that hotel was one of the first places that you all became a family.

AKC: That's exactly it. And it was just a haven. And while on the face of it, a pool and buffet doesn't sound that impactful, but just eating together there at the table—and we were there for three months, so a significant amount of time. They grew up in a place we all love, but is often chaotic. So when we had that family time around the pool, which was quieter and calmer, it was precious. (They also, of course, love Disneyland.)

DH: Share a travel story gone wrong.

AKC: In graduate school, a friend and I traveled to Mexico. And this is in the late nineties, so there was internet, but not really. We were trying to figure things out for the first night. My friend had picked this . . . not that great of a hotel for us to stay at. We got there and threw our stuff in the room, and then left. So someone broke in and stole her leather jacket with all her stuff in it. We got back and realized it was gone, and then when we went down to the lobby, and there was a guy wearing her jacket. It didn't make any sense—why would you wear a jacket around that you just stole—but anyway, we got it back and everything was fine.

DH: Well, that's a rough start to the trip.

AKC: That's the advantage to being young and maintaining that sort of outlook on things, because we didn't let it ruin the trip. We decided to go back out and try to erase the memory that evening. Something will always happen when you travel, but that's part of not trying to plan every little minute. It allows you to actually have random memories and funny experiences.

DH: How has travel changed you as a person?

AKC: It will sound really basic, but it's not to be underestimated: simply valuing and appreciating different perspectives and cultures. People and our environment are so interconnected. The decisions that we make have a domino effect. And if we can speak to each other and understand each other at a deeper level, it just enables greater collaboration and productivity. I just think you just need to have this appreciation for the world at large. And travel has allowed me to do that.

DH: Keep it up, and keep dragging your kids all over the place.

AKC: I will!

CHAPTER 7

EXPAND YOUR MIND

How Travel Changes You

We all grow up with some set of principles. It doesn't matter if you were raised in the heartland of America or the middle of Tokyo. This learned set of beliefs that we've gathered from our life experiences shapes who we are as individuals. What you believe drives how you behave in the world, the decisions you make, and the way you conduct yourself with others.

Travel is the single greatest thing you can do to expand your mind. When you go outside your comfort zone, you have no choice but to observe and learn about other ways of life. This is true whether you're crossing an ocean or just heading to a different neighborhood for dinner.

Most of the time, these changes are subconscious. It can take a few weeks of being back at home before you notice you might be seeing or reacting to things differently. But whatever your belief system is, I promise travel will force you to expand it.

Travel will change everything about you over time, if you keep it up—your taste in food and clothes, the art you appreciate, the choices you make as a consumer. It will make you a photographer, a journalist, and a pro at walking into a bar and striking up a conversation with a stranger—no matter how introverted you usually are.

It will make you a better listener, and more empathetic to your friends and family, not to mention some people you didn't think you liked. And it will give you stories for a lifetime of dinner parties—ones that people actually want to listen to!

Best of all, it puts everything in perspective. Challenges you face in everyday life will not seem as critical and important as they once did. If you lose your job and everything goes to shit, you can always start over on another continent, right?

People that you met on the road will come to visit you! One of the most rewarding parts of making friends in foreign countries is getting to return the favor one day.

Most important, after all the transformation you go through on the road, remember who you were raised to be, and consider how you can use those experiences to shape the world for the better.

Chase Jarvis

Chase literally wrote the book on creativity (*Creative Calling*, Harper Business, 2019). He's an award-winning photographer, shooting commercial campaigns for the likes of Apple, Nike, and The North Face. He's also the founder and CEO of CreativeLive, the world's largest platform for creative learning.

I idolized Chase as a university student and had the chance to meet him in 2011 when I got to participate in a live class on using still cameras for video creation. Chase grew up in a family that always made room in the budget for international travel. It transformed his life, and made him who he is today.

Daniel Houghton: So what I don't have in the book yet is any perspective from someone that makes his living the way you do it, as a photographer and a creative. Talk to me a little bit about what you're doing now. Then I'd love to hear whether you traveled when you were growing up. Was that something that was a part of your life?

Chase Jarvis: When I go back to my childhood, I grew up middle class. My mom was a secretary and I'm an only child. We were a tight-knit family. Starting when I was eleven or twelve we went to Europe once a year, even though we rarely had extra money. I had to wear two sweatshirts in the house because my mom kept the house at sixty degrees. She was very frugal with things, yet we would go to Europe. That had a completely transformational impact on me. Another reason we were able to afford it is because they were coming out with airline deals, my dad would take extra shifts at work—working concerts and sporting events. He was a cop for twenty-five years; you start to know all the people in the organization. Indirectly, our family became friends with sports stars.

My dad became friends with some of the players of the local soccer team here. A lot of them were European, British in particular. I remember our plane tickets being in the hundreds of dollars, and yet when we got there, these people that were playing on the international teams and top clubs would pick us up at the airport. So I had this amazing opportunity to go from this suburban kid life to basically the UK punk scene. It was such a departure from my little white middle-class suburban imagery.

DH: How lucky are you that your family made room in the budget for such fun and exploration.
CJ: Yeah. It gave me a sense of the world, a desire to connect with different cultures. Also, I think it inspired me to ensure that travel was a part of my professional experience when I decided to leave school. Then, a week before my college graduation, my grandfather, who was an avid photographer, dropped dead of a heart attack. Just completely out of the blue.

The silver lining was that he left me his cameras. And that kicked everything off. So I had planned, with financial gifts and the cameras, to go live out of a backpack and learn how to take pictures. My then-girlfriend, now-wife Kate and I went traipsing around Europe. It was really the alchemy of those things and, in particular, travel between major cities like Paris, Barcelona, Rome, Warsaw, and Budapest. This mix of pop culture in the cities and adventure travel—that is basically the life I have created for myself as a photographer. When action sports went mainstream, I had the opportunity to also go mainstream with my personal brand, and professionally with the work I was doing. You could make five hundred dollars a picture with a whiskey company and then five years later I would be making two hundred and fifty thousand with the same picture—just with a different dealer, because it would be an SUV company as opposed to a smaller company.

DH: Tell me about some of your favorite trips that you had to go on as part of shooting some of those campaigns and stuff. What are some of the interesting places that you got to go?
CJ: I think part of my joy was getting paid to research and go to some of the most remarkable places in the world, because that's what taking pictures, and specifically advertising, is about—creating an aspirational image. And so, as the photographer and the lead of these campaigns for these larger companies, it is my job to discover and then capture those insane adventures, with the goal of transporting people from their desk jobs to their wildest imaginations. Some require shots on six or seven different continents. The highest peaks in Africa, Alaska, the craziest shit you can imagine. On one campaign, for an undisclosed running shoe company, we visited the eleven destinations of the Olympic Torch Relay—in marathon fashion. We would fly to a location, shoot first light on the marathon course, pack up, and get on a plane to the next country. And we circumnavigated the globe in seventeen days, I think. That's just the tip of the iceberg. You go anywhere with an unlimited helicopter budget.

You go somewhere like New Zealand, you get to experience everything—the beaches, the cities, and everything in between. Amazing food, history, and an indigenous culture. And by getting paid to explore those, to document them, to share them, and bring the rest of the world with you, and share the things that you found with the rest of the world . . . it's impossible to quantify the impact it had on me personally. And I think being able to experience that as a photographer certainly inspired me to want to help others pursue their most audacious goals. You know, you start traveling with your girlfriend and you get paid to take pictures in Europe and you say, "My God, is it possible to make a living doing this?" And if I can do it, it's my belief that anyone could.

DH: Tell me about a place that you went to that wasn't how you imagined it. Have you had any experiences like that?
CJ: Oh sure. So many. Africa comes to mind. Just the vastness. Maybe you're down in Cape Town and experience so much history and racial divide, and then be embedded with all of those cultures, even for a short period of time, on a life scale, it is transformative—seeing how we really are all the same. We have different meanings, different tools, different languages, but at our core, the love that a mother has for a child or that a family has is the same—it's universal. Africa certainly captures that. South America also. I've spent a lot of time in the southern hemisphere. Those indigenous cultures, which you may initially feel disconnected from because of language and culture, food—but then you spend some time in them and find these beautiful, heartwarming stories of human connection . . . I think that's the thing with photography—there are 7,106 languages in the world, you know; that means there are 7,106 ways to say "I love you," 7,106 ways to say "I'm sorry," or "Will you marry me?"—to say everything there is to say, and yet, if I show you a photograph—for example,

a mother with a newborn child—every culture understands that photograph intuitively and instantly. There's this universality to photography; it can transcend race, religion, gender, orientation, culture, even time. We're lucky to have tapped into something universal.

DH: Universally accepted.
CJ: Yeah. I'm thinking about the book that you're writing, I think that's the most powerful insight I can offer—how a single image of a stand-alone thing, whether it's manipulated, shared, or not, is this very, very powerful connective tissue, because it can tell a story about another culture without your having to go there and see it for yourself.

DH: Right. Absolutely. That's amazing. I always tried, when I was working as a photojournalist, to get in touch with people I had spent time with in foreign countries and give them pictures. I can't tell you how many times something as simple as remembering to email someone a photo came back tenfold later. There are so many places in the world I could land and have a place to stay, just because I gave someone a picture of their family.
CJ: Yeah, I think that's it. It's so acceptable now, not like when we were shooting slide film twenty years ago and we had to develop it in a lab in a city. The ability to communicate or share that image immediately now as a mechanism of connection—obviously, the times have changed.

This is such a cool topic, especially now, when the media portrays the world as sort of violent and scary and divided, and yet the facts—the murder rate, infant mortality, all these things are the best they have ever been in the history of the universe. The number of people that have been lifted out of poverty or gained access to clean drinking water in the last ten years, it's remarkable.

DH: It's unbelievable.

CJ: And so to have a vehicle to help shed some light on that, I think is really cool. That's part of what both photographs and the written word can do. I look at it as an obligation; we have to tell stories.

Noo Saro-Wiwa

Noo Saro-Wiwa is an author, freelance journalist, and one of *Conde Nast Traveler*'s "world's most influential female travelers." Her first book, *Looking for Transwonderland: Travels in Nigeria*, was published by Soft Skull in 2012.

The title was selected as BBC Radio 4's Book of the Week, and the *Sunday Times* Travel Book of the Year, among many other honors.

Noo Saro-Wiwa: Hi, how are you?

Daniel Houghton: Doing very well. Thank you for taking the time for this on a weekend. I don't think I realized until after I contacted you that you actually used to write guidebooks for Lonely Planet.
NS: I did. Well, I did it for one edition in 2003.

DH: Let's talk travel!
NS: I was born in Nigeria and raised in England. After I graduated, I got my first travel gig with Rough Guides. So I went to Guinea with them. And that was really the making of me, that trip. That was my first experience backpacking around Africa by myself. I would never have written my book without doing that. And then I worked for ABC News, the American affiliate in London, as a production research assistant. I then went to Columbia University to study journalism for one year. And it was there that I realized I definitely didn't want to become a reporter, a news reporter—which had always been my plan.

DH: Right. Mine as well.

NS: I realized I wanted to write stories, but in book form, and stories that didn't usually make the headlines. So I returned to ABC for another year just to make some money, then went to South Africa, to write what would have been my first book. I declined to a publishing deal for it in the end. But it was a really great experience. And then I decided to work for Lonely Planet—went to five countries in Africa including: Madagascar, Ghana, Togo, Benin. And then I wrote what turned out to be my first published book, which was *Looking for Transwonderland: Travels in Nigeria* (Soft Skull Press, August 2012).

My father was a human rights activist and environmentalist. And he was killed by the military dictatorship in the mid-nineties. So I hadn't been back to Nigeria much since then. And it was a very personal mission, to explore the country in a way that just made me hate it less, you know, and disassociate it from my father's memory.

DH: Did you know that one day you'd go back home in some capacity? Was that something you had planned? Or did writing kind of open the door into that for you?

NS: Yeah. When I worked for Lonely Planet, they suggested that I go to Nigeria to cover it, and I was like, "No way. I don't want to go to Nigeria." But after having spent about a year in South Africa writing that book, I had second thoughts. And you know, South Africa is so different from Nigeria, it's like being in California or something.

DH: Yeah. I've been to South Africa, a little bit, just there, and a stopover in Senegal. But other than that, I haven't spent

much time in Africa. I only know enough to know that it's like visiting many different continents.

NS: Yeah, definitely. I mean because I covered all these countries in West Africa, I had a feeling of what traveling around Nigeria would be like. But it's something you can actually do as a tourist, the same way I went to Ghana and all these other places. And yeah, I find it easier to deal with hardship when you know that all that hardship becomes material for a book.

DH: You obviously got a lot of critical acclaim for that book. And I know a lot of people got in touch with you after that, saying the book opened their eyes. Did you expect that? Or was it a surprise?

NS: I mean, for me, writing is about sharing your experiences, and you hope for the people who read about your experiences to react in the same way you did. So for me, travel writing is about exploring something new and then sharing that excitement with other people.

DH: And it must be a thrill to realize you have the power to do that. I know you're very interested in China—I'd love to hear about the other places you've been. What are some of your favorites, and why?

NS: I think every country has something different—there aren't that many countries that satisfy me on all counts. But I went to Uzbekistan, in 2017, for a newspaper travel piece, and that really blew me away. I've never been that far.

DH: Did you have a perception of what Uzbekistan would be like?

NS: Yeah, I guess my assumptions were just based on what I'd seen, you kind of have a sense of what people look like, what the major tourist attractions are. I was only there for eight days, it was a pressed trip. But, you know, no matter how much you read about a place and watch videos, there's nothing like experiencing it for real. So it was seeing these faces, so beautiful, that kind of mix of Persian and Chinese and Russian. I was taking endless photos and portraits of people, and of the Persian architecture. To stand at the bottom of these mosques—it's really hard to describe, you just have to kind of be there to see it. And also, they were really friendly. You're never sure, especially as an African, how people are going to perceive you, but I was really pleasantly surprised. I mean, I just got the rock star treatment. It was amazing.

DH: Wow.
NS: Everywhere I went, people were smiling. People saying hello, wanting to take selfies. It just made the whole experience really nice. I had never been to that part of the world, that crossroads of Asia, Europe, and Central Asia. So that had a big impact on me. It wasn't a country I had thought a lot about going to.

DH: What part of China fascinates you the most? If you could get on a plane tomorrow, what part of China would you go back to?
NS: It wouldn't be the south, because that is where I spent most of my time. I would like to explore the more northern areas. The Chinese diaspora, you know, mostly came from the south. So I'm used to that kind of China. My Malaysian friends, Singaporean friends, Hong Kong friends—they're all from those southern provinces.

DH: And that part doesn't seem as unfamiliar to us, I think.

NS: No, even on a phonetic level. So when I went to, let's see, what was the first northern province? Shanxi Province. That was the first northern province I'd been to, and I was really shocked at how people spoke. I'm so used to asking for things in Chinese and southern Hong Kong—Cantonese, basically. And the whole accent was different—the way they roll their *r*'s, almost like Irish Americans. And I was like, "Wow, this is just completely different." So yeah, I'd like to explore more of northern China. Xinjiang Province looks amazing, in the far northwest. Really beautiful national parks and waterfalls and things. And again, that sort of Persian, Central Asian feeling to it, like Uzbekistan. I really like that aesthetic. So I'd love to go to northwest China.

DH: As a journalist, let me ask you this. What do you think humanity's opinion on travel is at the moment? Admittedly, I'm an optimist, but I just can't help believing that if everyone had the opportunity to travel, even just a little bit, it would immediately cure a lot of issues, which is why I'm writing this book.

NS: Yeah, I mean, I think there are a lot of people who travel for the wrong reason. So I think there are people who aren't actually interested in travel. I don't think you should force people into it. If they get on a plane and go thousands of miles just to hang out with people who are very similar to them and not really explore, then I really feel people like that shouldn't travel.

DH: Right.

NS: Traveling doesn't have to be far.

DH: Absolutely agree.

NS: I mean, we do live in an amazing era, and it may not last forever. So I want to make the most of it. And I think, for the developed parts of the world, travel is getting cheaper. It's more accessible, which comes with problems if you flock to the same places as everyone else. I feel everywhere has an interesting story. But you have to dig a little deeper, you know, and in this day and age, it's not enough to just go to Egypt and say, "Oh, I saw a pyramid."

And even though the world is converging culturally, in lots of ways, I still think that every country expresses in its own unique way. The smallest town and the most boring parts of any country are full of exciting stuff, but you have to go look for it. And yeah, it is really important to travel. I find simply going to a country you've never been to before, you suddenly engage with it in a different way, you come back home, and suddenly the newspaper articles about that country that you used to ignore, suddenly you're paying attention, because you've been there. And that's a small step towards helping people engage with different parts of the world.

DH: How has travel changed you as a person? You had such a unique upbringing—you probably encountered more cultures before you were eighteen than most people do in a lifetime. How do you feel like your explorations have changed you and helped you as a person?
NS: Well, the thing about travel is it forces you out of your comfort zone, because you're in a place where you may not understand the language, you don't know how things work. And so you have to speak to people more, you have to ask questions, you have to get help from people. And obviously, people approach you and make conversation in a way that they don't at home. And so that kind of brought me out of my shell. It also helped me realize that

we're all the same fundamentally. And I think a lot of people don't understand that. Today people are seeing all these images on TV, of African migrants coming over on boats . . .

DH: And they think, they can't possibly be like I am? Yeah.
NS: Exactly. But if they traveled to the actual countries where they come from, they would know that's not the case. And it's such a huge divide we find within humanity, those who travel and those who don't. Their perceptions of things like the migrant crisis are radically different.

Because you have to seek advice from strangers when you travel, it makes you much better at judging people's character, because as a female traveler, you want to avoid the guy who's going to come on to you or something. And as an African, you sort of gauge whether someone is going to be rude to you, just by looking at them.

DH: Yeah, you don't know what stereotypes they're harboring, right?
NS: Yeah. So I've become much better at observing people—gestures and facial movements, things like that. And I've learned to trust people more. And as I said, it helps you realize that the vast majority of people are incredibly helpful, very decent.

DH: On a more lighthearted note, I would love to hear what you do when you get to a place for the first time. Do you research places heavily before you go? Are you really organized, or do you fly by the seat of your pants?
NS: Yeah, it's interesting. To me, things have changed over the years. You're a lot younger than me, but when I was traveling in

my early twenties, that was the late nineties. So technology hadn't really taken off yet. So I relied on guidebooks a lot more. And I would read, that was all part of my preparation. Because you weren't looking at loads of photos online.

Sometimes, you know, it's the best way to explore. The best experiences have come through serendipity rather than having plans.

DH: A lot of my travels have been only three or four days at a time, and I have to hope that the stars will align for me to come back someday. But you've spent much longer periods of time abroad. Is that right?
NS: Yeah. The big ones are China, Africa, Nigeria, because I've written books about them.

DH: And how did those experiences differ for you? Obviously, more time is going to open your eyes in a much different way. But do you have a preference?
NS: I think, honestly, I prefer staying longer; I get much more out of it. My least interesting travel experiences have been the ones that have been pure vacation brain. So you know, I went to the Philippines purely for vacation and it was all very peaceful and everything.

DH: You're there to relax, not to dive in full steam. And that's okay, I think.
NS: It's okay, but it's a bit weird. What I'm finding now is, I'd much rather go with a friend who lives in that country. Especially if you only have three or four days, exploring with somebody who actually lives there or is from there can be so much better than kicking around by yourself for a month. And I find that the older you get, the more friends you have around the world. So these

days, I've half given up the idea of going to places on vacation, I just feel like I'll get there eventually, one way or another. For example, I went on a writer's retreat in Italy for a month with a bunch of other people from different parts of the world. And it was amazing. We all bonded. So now I suddenly have a new friend who's Egyptian and one who's Brazilian. And you know, I've never been to South America apart from Brazil.

DH: Oh wow.

NS: This Brazilian guy, his boyfriend is Peruvian. And then another lady was Colombian. And so it's like, "Okay, this is the reason why I've never been to South America. The travel gods were just waiting for me to make friends."

DH: Right. And now I'm going to have such a better time because I've got someone to call when I hit the ground. Tell me about any upcoming places that you're going anytime in the next year that you've never been to before. Or maybe you have, but you're excited to return.

NS: Well, I'm going to Pakistan, with a friend from school. We've known each other for twenty-odd years. And she's from the northern parts of Pakistan—in the mountains. They have a home there. And so I'm going to visit and then write about it for the *Financial Times* travel section. So I'm really excited about that. I've never been to the subcontinent at all. I never imagined I'd be going to Pakistan before I ever got to India.

DH: Yeah.

NS: My book just got translated into Italian, so I go to Italy a lot. I love Italy. Something about Sicily, it's just one of my favorite places. And then Venice, which I haven't been to since I was a kid. So that'll be interesting. Should be a lot of fun. And then I'm doing a workshop in Zanzibar in July.

DH: Oh, wow.
NS: Yeah, I've never been there.

DH: That's great.
NS: Oh, and there's an organization trying to revitalize a national park in Nigeria. So I'll be going to that later on in the year. But that's a long story!

CHAPTER 8

JUST GO!

Travel is more accessible than ever before.

> "All you've got to do is decide to go, and the hardest
> part is over."—Tony Wheeler

Actually, the cofounder of Lonely Planet has so many inspiring quotes on why we should all get out and see the world that it's damn hard to choose just one. Luckily, I've interviewed Tony for this book, so you'll get to hear more.

I want to take a few minutes and just implore you to book a trip while you're reading this book. I want to show you just how easy it is to make the decision to leave your house and go experience the world.

To understand just how good we have it, let's examine the royal pain in the ass that planning and booking travel used to be. Travel agents, brochures, long waits on hold while trying to call airlines. Most of the time, you had to book hotels or houses sight

unseen, leading to some unwelcome surprises. Visas, passport re-
newals, and tour reservations had to be done months in advance,
often by mail. Some places were only reachable by a handful of
flights, so woe to you if you missed one.

The experience today couldn't be more different. It doesn't matter if you're broke, only have two days off from work, have never left
your home country, or are terrified of how you're ever going to be
able to get where you're going, there's a website with directions—
and solutions—waiting for you. We are living in a world where we
can ask a smart speaker in our kitchen, "Hey Google/Alexa/Siri,
how much are flights to Hong Kong?" and get an answer in seconds.

It takes about forty-five seconds to find those answers to
get to almost anywhere on earth, minus the last-mile problem if
you're going somewhere truly out of the way. The most restricting
thing about travel is usually the cost.

But once you're armed with the information to make a decision on just how badly you want to drain your bank account, the
genuine fun begins. There are literally millions if not billions of
Google search results to help you plan a trip to just about anywhere on earth.

Need advice on what to do when you arrive? Head over to
Lonely Planet, *Condé Nast Traveler*, the *New York Times* travel
section, Matador Network, or any of the millions of incredible
travel blogs spread across the internet.

Want to find the cheapest flights? It's hard to beat Google
Flights for quick flight results, but also check Kayak, Booking
.com, Expedia, or Ctrip. Or get a little crazy and check the airline's website directly!

Where are you going to stay when you arrive? Head over
to Booking.com for the most global results and best prices but

also check places like HotelTonight or Airbnb, Expedia, and HomeAway.

You can successfully plan an international excursion in less than an hour these days—and go with a confidence that previous generations couldn't have dreamed of. Everyone I interviewed for this book shared at least one story of a trip gone horribly wrong, but except for Richard Branson's near-death experiences (he has a bit of a unique and dangerous way of traveling), the worst thing that happened was a stolen bag or phone, and even those stories were rare.

If you're worried about not speaking the language when you hit the ground, there have never been more free resources for picking up a second language. It's hard to beat the Duolingo app if you're serious about conversing with locals. If you're a little less adventurous and just need to know enough to get around on the ground, check out the Guides by Lonely Planet app for iOS or Android—there are free travel phrase books for more than fifteen languages.

A lot of people get hung up on travel planning once they pass the point of figuring out general cost and transportation. The detail logistics of travel can seem daunting, but they too have never been easier. With Uber, Lyft, and other ride-sharing companies expanding to most of the developed world, ground transportation is covered. You can even estimate costs on those platforms before you ever book your tickets, to get a total picture of your trip's finances.

My advice? Don't get too worried about what you're going to do when you hit the ground. Most of the fun in travel lies in the unknown. Get there, venture out of your hotel, and just go for a walk. I guarantee what you find by accident will surpass any piece of travel or destination advice you can find online or get from a friend.

When I land someplace new, I typically have done about an hour or two of total research just to get some idea of places I might want to visit when I'm wandering around. Don't feel like you have to plan every minute of your trip; just make it up as you go along.

I'm often reading Wikipedia entries on the plane while we are headed to the gate. Anything you can learn about local culture and customs will benefit you along the way.

Challenge yourself to go somewhere you didn't think you would ever be comfortable. Afraid to go to Asia because you don't speak the local language? People are pretty friendly on the road. Don't be scared to ask for directions or help. You may or may not want to follow the advice of the hotel staff, but in places where not many speak your language, the hotel staff has the best shot at helping you if you hit the ground without a plan.

Wander around and take a few minutes to reflect on the fact that you made it. You got off the couch, got on the plane, and now you're there!

Smile a lot, make friends, and keep detailed notes so when you decide to return, you already have people to see and things to do.

Travel until all that is foreign becomes familiar!

Laura Dekker

On August 1, 2010, Laura Dekker left the Netherlands in a thirty-eight-foot sailboat and spent 518 days circumnavigating the planet—at the age of sixteen, becoming the youngest person in history to do so solo.

She authored a book, *One Girl One Dream*, about her journey, which I implore you to read. She's a speaker and professional sailboat captain, and also runs a foundation dedicated to inspiring others to travel.

Daniel Houghton: Hey, thank you for making the time. Sorry about the delay. You're in Europe currently?
Laura Dekker: Yes.

DH: I'd love to just hear a little bit about you and how you grew up. And what made you want to travel in the first place? Was travel always a part of your life?
LD: Sure. Yes, I did travel a lot with my parents. My parents were actually sailing around the world while I was born. So that's why I was born in New Zealand. After we sailed back to Holland, my parents divorced, and I just kind of decided to stay with my dad, who was building a new boat. So for a little while, we lived in a caravan right next to the boats. And then, when the boat was turned around, we could actually live in it onshore. And I went in the water and almost drowned. So yeah, I guess from six to thirteen, we were living on the boat in Holland—still traveling, but not, like, world traveling.

DH: So it's safe to say that the boat has always been a very comfortable place for you. It's not like you grew up in a house and one day decided you wanted to go sailing.

LD: Ha ha, no. I knew I wanted to do this.

DH: Other than, obviously, your big trip, tell me about some of the other places you've been. Which ones have stuck out over the years?

LD: Well, what makes travel so special for me is to see so many places, and realize that not one is perfect. And there are problems everywhere. But there's also beauty everywhere. When you travel, you actually get an overview and realize that—at least for me—it doesn't really matter how I live or what I do, because everybody does it differently. So it's important to stay yourself and to be happy with that.

DH: Talk for a few minutes about that big trip. Was that something that you had been planning for a long time?

LD: Well, it was a dream of mine from when I was probably seven or eight. I never really thought about how or when until later. For me, it was about travel and seeing the world, not about the records. And I guess I just left when I felt ready. I did this trip to England, and then I came back and just really had a strong feeling that was the right time.

DH: And you made a couple stops along the way, right? You spent long periods in basically complete isolation. Talk to me about what it was like to go from that to popping back into big cities. Was that very jarring?

LD: I always find jumping back really hard. I liked it a lot better out

at sea. So coming back just made me realize that I'm looking from another view, a different perspective from everyone else. I felt like the world was racing around, and I was just standing still. I think when you're in the rat race, you don't really see it, but when you step outside of it for a while, you kind of think, "What is all this for?"

DH: So, pretty hard to rejoin society.
LD: It is very difficult. Yes.

DH: These days, when you decide that you need to take a break, do you go back out on the boat and spend some time by yourself? What's your escape?
LD: Sailing. I also read or write. I play an instrument. I really like music, but yeah, nothing does it quite like sailing for me.

DH: When you finished that massive trip, you were still a teenager. What were the next couple of years like? How did that experience shape who you've ended up becoming as a person?
LD: Good question. Um, I think I always grew up quite differently. I had a strong sense that I should reach my goals and fight for them. I had never really been in "society" the same way other people have. So because of that, I didn't really know how to get back in, or I never really tried.

I just kept doing my own thing, and I did travel a lot and got my captain's license, because I really wanted that, and then did some deliveries. Eventually, as the years went on, I realized how much I'd learned that other teenagers won't ever get to experience—things that I think would be super-valuable for people to just learn or see once. So I wished I had some way to pass it on.

That's what my new project is about. I want to build a big boat, and take kids sailing on it. But I don't want to teach sailing, I want to teach life lessons. I want them to actually do everything themselves on the boat—they should sail it, clean up, do the dishes and the cooking, and work with each other. I think it's important to learn that you're actually much more capable of things than people tell you. In schools you're taught to follow a system, a particular path. And some people function very well in that system, but others don't function at all. And they're just like a withering flower that sits depressed.

They don't know how to get themselves going again, because they never learned it. And I was very fortunate to grow up with parents that did understand how I saw things, and what I needed. So I really want to pass that on further.

DH: Yeah, I couldn't agree more. I was never very good at following the system. I really struggled in school—not that I was a bad kid, but for me the classroom was not a way to learn.

Travel was one of the only things that made sense to me. So I felt very lucky that I could make a living at it, because I barely got out of high school and university.
LD: Everybody learns very differently. But I do think that learning in practice, by actually doing stuff, works the fastest. Some people really need that. Give them the opportunity.

DH: How do you think your adventures have shaped who you are as a person? For me, it radically opened my mind, which I think is true for most people. But there were definitely some specific ways I changed—from becoming less of a picky eater to being more comfortable walking up and talking to strangers.

LD: Yeah, of course. Many experiences, I guess. Travel always shapes you a lot—you get to know yourself and you realize things about yourself that you probably wouldn't have otherwise because you're comfortable at home. I think the people that I met along the way probably had the biggest impact on me.

Of course, I did sail with my parents, but I don't remember a whole lot of that. So most of what I had seen and knew from my childhood was Europe, and Western society, where everything is about becoming the best, having the biggest house and the biggest car. And for me, it was really beautiful to see islands where people were just living in little huts, but actually freely happy. Just to realize that, you know, all these things that I've heard in school aren't necessarily true.

So that was a really important lesson, to just be happy with what you've got. The boat itself also taught me that, in a certain way. But the friendliness of people on these little islands, and the fact that they really, actually listen and care, which is also something that is hard to find these days. Those were the moments that I thought, "Okay, I want to keep that forever and take it with me and apply it."

Stephen Mansfield

Stephen is a *New York Times* bestselling author, speaker, advisor to governments, and world traveler. He also runs the Mansfield Group, a media company based in Washington, DC. As I reviewed the list of who I had interviewed for this book, I realized I had no input on how the world's religions have driven people to travel since the beginning of time. Stephen joins us to share a fascinating perspective on the history of travel, as well as his own experiences abroad.

Daniel Houghton: Stephen, it's great to have you as a part of this book. Tell us a little bit about yourself.
Stephen Mansfield: I started my professional life with twenty years of pastoring. The second ten years was at Belmont Church in Nashville when it was about a four- to five-thousand-member church. Then I transitioned out of that—I am the kind of guy who knew he would be a pastor for half of his life but not all of his life—and immediately began to dive deeper into writing.

I had written some books before that had won awards, but then I had a couple of *New York Times* best sellers. One was *The Faith of George W. Bush.* This did exactly what I'd hoped it would do—it repositioned me for the second part of my life, which has to do with engaging culture more directly, working internationally, starting organizations, consulting, a lot of media, things like that. In other words, just speaking to the issues that are critical in our culture.

So my life is divided between twenty years of travel as a pastor, as a guy overseeing social service organizations, and as a speaker.

Then the second twenty years is as an author, a guy that consults with pretty high-level government circles and does a lot of business speaking.

DH: Talk to me about travel for you and how that started. Was that something you did with your parents? Was that something you ended up doing on your own as part of your job?

SM: Travel was an important part of my life from the beginning. My father was an army officer. This was back in the day when the military was a little less aware of the impact that moving around had on the families. So we moved almost every year for all of my first eighteen years—that was fairly typical. My parents were very good at making it exciting. Believe it or not, we'd travel with an entire set of encyclopedias in the back of our station wagon.

So, if you're driving through Louisiana and you see a sign that says "something parish," my mom would go, "Huh, wonder why they are called parishes and not counties?" And sure enough, one of us would race to that volume and find out. And wherever we were, they made sure we went and saw things. When we were stationed in Virginia, we went to Williamsburg, we went to DC, we went to Gettysburg, we went to Mount Vernon. They were really good about that. And of course, we were stationed twice in Germany—once in Berlin. That was Berlin during the Cold War. So at the time, of course, the city was divided—French, British, Russian, etc. It was an extremely multicultural situation. There were Communists on the other side of the wall. I went to an American high school there, and we traveled all over Europe to compete in athletics. So those were my early experiences.

If you want to move on quickly to the professional, my biggest travel period was when I became the senior staff member at Belmont Church in Nashville. And I helped that church grow to a point where it spent one-third of its budget on missions. That was pretty rare then. But that was just the kind of church it was. So now I'm going to Iraqi Kurdistan because we had a huge outreach with the Kurds—not just with missions, but advocating for them.

I even testified before Congress about supporting the Kurds. But then we also had missionaries all over the world that I would visit and hold events for during those years. Papua New Guinea, Uzbekistan, Thailand, several places in the Middle East, Pakistan, etc.

DH: Could you give me a quick history lesson, including the religious aspects, on the origins of travel?
SM: Yeah, it's interesting. In the early, early days of human history, when you're talking largely about the pagan world—the pre-Jewish, pre-Christian world—travel was inhibited a bit by the idea that gods were local. So you had the XYZ people, for example, and the XYZ people worshipped the pillow god, and the pillow god had a forty-mile reach in every direction. And you didn't want to get outside the reach of the pillow god, because you wouldn't have power, or you wouldn't be protected. Later, as trade began to open up and individual regions began to flower or become known for certain benefits, people got a little bit more adventurous. And on the heels of that came religious travel.

In the Roman era, of course, basic roads were built and protected over almost all of the known world. And so traveling was vast and huge, and largely for religious reasons. The Jews hadn't traveled that much, except to captivity and for trade. But by the time you get to the Christian world, travel is huge. Even just following one biblical figure, like Paul in the New Testament, it's almost an exhausting array of travel.

And of course, missions continue today. There are even gigantic churches in the world that have their own planes. That's not just for the pastor to go out to dinner in other cities, that's to go around the world rapidly.

DH: Fascinating. How do you personally feel about modern religious organizations and their missions? Is that better than it's ever been, or is it more difficult because of the political climate?
SM: No, I think in terms of religious organizations, churches, synagogues, we're at an apex in history for traveling. And it's not just for missionary purposes. There's a lot of educational travel.

It's not uncommon at all to have a plane full of Jews flying from New York to study in South American synagogues. And of course, trips to Israel, or to Europe right now to help fight anti-Semitism. It would be rare to start to look at a Christian or a Jewish or even a Muslim university and not find extensive travel for educational purposes. That would not have been happening two generations ago. So I think it's a high point, in fact. And of course, missions are now allowed in most of the world. In a way, there's more religious persecution than ever—but in a very small percentage of countries, and the rest are becoming more cosmopolitan.

For the most part, religious people are allowed to travel anywhere they want and talk to anybody they want. And of course, over the recent generations, the cost of travel has come down to where the average person can afford it—a ditch digger, a truck driver, a bartender. At least in the United States, and probably, if they are careful, anywhere in the world. So those two trends have made an absolute cornucopia of travel for the average religious person today.

DH: I know you've been a lot of places over the years. But one of the things I read about was that you were embedded with troops during the Iraq War. That's right?
SM: Yes.

DH: That had to be a different travel experience for you. What can you share with me about that? I feel like a lot of people that join the military have the opportunity to travel that they never had before.
SM: Yeah, it was absolutely fascinating. It was 2005, I was at Camp Victory in Iraq. The trip itself was interesting. Because I fly a lot, and almost exclusively on Delta, I'm able to upgrade myself. So I'm flying first-class to Europe. I get to Paris and I get on a Middle East Airlines flight in first class and fly to Kuwait City. Got to Kuwait City, immediately went to a military facility and got on a C130. And then we flew into Iraq. At one point the pilot came on and said, "We are going in for the landing, so strap in." You're sitting and facing the center of the plane, not the front. It was basically a combat zone landing—an interesting transition from first class. Then you get off the plane, you have your helmet on, they are yelling at you like your mother saying they just had some engagement on the edge of the airfield.

So being there was tricky, and you notice how quickly people come and go from the battlefield now. You know, years ago, you put a guy in Vietnam, and he would leave for R&R just once the entire year or two years there. Maybe meet his wife in Hawaii. But from Iraq, a guy could fly to Kuwait or even Germany just over the weekend to have a medical procedure and come back. Senior officers routinely flew back to Washington, DC. And they got on the plane and came back and they hardly knew they were gone. So anyway, the sheer volume of travel is stunning. But having grown up in the military, you know that you are dealing with people from all over the world.

It really is a joining or gathering of cultures that is as fascinating as any place in the world. And there, we weren't just American forces at war, we were a coalition at war. At Camp Victory, I sat there with Aussies, New Zealanders, Germans, and officers, and military chaplains, everyone, with various languages and accents and cultural issues.

DH: What did you observe in some of the men and women who were enlisted over there? I assume for many of them that was the first time they had been out of the country, and for others, just another deployment. Talk to me a little bit about why you were there. Was this for book research?

SM: Yeah, I wrote a book called *The Faith of the American Soldier*— it was all about what we were hearing at that time. You're probably aware of soldiers getting baptized in the sands of Iraq. There was a low-grade religious revival going on there. So the question was, "What would it be for this generation?" Because this generation was a little less Christian. A little less churchy. A little more nontraditional. But everyone is set on a religious journey when they are at war. Believe it or not, the soldiers in this war were older and more educated than previous generations.

DH: It wasn't just eighteen-year-olds like in Vietnam.

SM: Right. Many of them were reserve, and they had gone into the reserves to get scholarships for college. They never thought they would go to war. So they were a few clicks older, and better educated. There was also an evident divide between the hard-core soldiers and the reserves—the twenty-one-year-old who was in biology class six months ago. And that's a big difference—another way that travel creates a cultural mix.

When I said goodbye to my father during Vietnam, we half expected him to die. But these folks could very well be home in six months, and back in biology class. That would have been inconceivable in the Vietnam era. The guys sat at the airport for two weeks when they wanted to get out of there. And so as a result of that kind of speed, and the modern tools that allow you to stay connected to your own culture (iPods were huge while I was embedded in Iraq)—it's not a professional-soldier type of transition. I talked to a girl who had just come back in from a Humvee, having been sprayed by an IED, seen a friend die, and shot up the enemy. But three nights ago she was in Germany dancing at a disco because she was there for a medical procedure. This kind of thing just didn't happen in World War II, Vietnam, or Korea. So again, travel transformed this battlefield.

DH: I doubt you had any time to spend with the locals on that trip, but was there a time when you did, there or in another conflict zone? Did it open up your eyes a bit? Any local stories that had a big impact on you?

SM: I actually did a lot of that because, in my early years of going to Kurdistan to work with the Kurds, there was a war going on. What's interesting about war zones is that there is almost always a full civilian world going on. It's almost removed from the war.

DH: And probably less affected than most people think.
SM: You're not just lined up on a battlefield charging at each other. I have gone to Iraqi homes, I have sat in restaurants while troops go carefully creeping by the window, crouched over and their guns raised, looking for insurgents. And I'm sitting in that window, by the way, with those Iraqi friends. You just feel weird. I've been awakened at night by the gunfire in the street. I've also been awakened and been handed a machine gun.

It was a big education for me, to see this world where yeah, sometimes you're on the battlefield, but for the most part, especially in Iraq, they had me teaching in churches, speaking at university, watching TV with a family and having dinner, holding babies. Of course technically you could die any minute, but it's not likely; it's more of an inconvenience. And I imagine the same thing went on during Vietnam. There are parts of Saigon that look the same as they did thirty years before anybody started shooting at each other.

We did come across a couple of firefights. They happened at the borders, tracer fire overhead, you just waited it out. I relate best to the journalists that we see on TV that work over there, that are suddenly killed. Because you can get, not careless per se, but casual.

DH: Well, you start to feel more comfortable. Not that you'd be completely comfortable in a conflict area, but I can see how it could start to feel safe. And you can start to kind of feel normal. You almost have to, after a while.
SM: Yeah, the "Let's meet for a drink over at the American Bar," or whatever is a very common experience. And when that bar

blows up, we are all in a state of shock and horrified at the loss of that journalist we loved—as we should be, by the way. All I'm saying is that it's not that anyone got casual, it's that the war suddenly invaded an otherwise pretty normal life.

DH: Yeah, absolutely. I want to talk a little bit about travel by government leaders. You've written books on politicians and presidents. Do you have a sense of how travel has impacted them as people, or how it's impacted the presidency?

SM: Yeah. I think the thing that always amazes me about that whole scene is the reality distortion field that happens with elite travel. Not so much Air Force One exclusively, but I've also traveled a lot with upper-level CEOs and business leaders. I'm just going to call it elite—where people really take care of you. The disconnect from a normal travel experience is huge.

I mean once the guy is president, the guy is never going to walk on the streets of the village again. But that's unfortunate, in some ways. So I do both. What happens at those upper levels is that you start to sound out of touch, not really making much sense to the guy on the street, not really understanding the situation on the ground. I'm just very aware that when Air Force One lands in a town, it's an invading army.

DH: Right. They are bringing all of the vehicles, all of the motorcade comes along. I don't think most Americans know that. They basically bring a battlefield with them everywhere.

SM: Exactly. So you have the press footage of Air Force One landing alone, but they don't show the F-14s overhead or the Secret Service that show up like an army or the C-130s that show up a week before.

DH: Indeed. Tell me a little bit about you when you travel. I'd love to hear some places that are still on your list to go, and what's your routine when you turn up in a new place. I try to get lost on purpose. It's pretty hard to get lost in reality, with our phones, but I try to just go for a walk and go in the direction of whatever interests me. Are there any habits like that when you get to a new place?

SM: Yeah, my desire is pretty similar to yours in that I just want to lose myself. My favorite moments are just sitting with Israeli guards and having them laugh and slap each other around, including me— everyone forgetting that I'm not Israeli. I like to blend in, I like to get lost, I like to sit in fields, I like to argue and talk and have fun and have them ask me questions and have it get rowdy. I like that culture. The tricky thing for me with travel is that I'm a pretty big guy. I'm somewhere between six-four and six-five and about 270 pounds right now, so there is no way I'm going to look local in a lot of places.

DH: Yeah, you're not going to blend.

SM: But yeah, I like to immediately get into the culture. But sometimes in order to do it, I play the American that doesn't know very much.

DH: Right. You have to or they are never going to stop wondering about you.

SM: And if you look at all athletic they think you are CIA or something. What does this American want? The art of travel for me when I'm in a foreign culture is I try to look smaller than I am. I step off the curb to talk to someone and stuff like that. I hunch down a little bit. I ask them, "Can you help the stupid American, or the silly American, understand?"

The most exciting and most informative moments I've had enlisting help are in the Middle East, where there is tremendous hospitality. I've literally had men just take my hand and walk me down the street to where their cousin owns the shop. And then they ask the cousin, "Where should he go for this?"—and now I've got five of them taking me through the streets of Damascus. Most of my extensive travel, both adventure and business, has been in the Muslim world. And I have somewhat of an academic specialty with Islam, so my biggest revelations, my biggest excitements, my most thrilling opportunities have been in the Muslim world, where there's often at least some kind of danger afoot. But there is also something gracious and welcoming, and hospitable.

DH: Certainly.

SM: I've spoken to terrorists, I've spoken to Hamas leaders. I mean none of this is that big of a deal, any journalist in that part of the world has these opportunities. But it continues to be the biggest revelation for me, that almost any blanket statement about "what Muslims think" is wrong. Almost any assumption even about extremist Islam is wrong. And so that has been my biggest education, my most fun, my best meals and best memories.

DH: Right. Thank you for sharing that, that's amazing. Picking up on your point, what do you think humanity's opinion on travel is at the moment? Are places like the Middle East safe? Are those cultures traveling more? Does the rest of the world have the view that America is sort of closed? Or is that mostly manufactured on the evening news?

SM: Yeah, I think the answer is that the world is divided between those who travel and those who don't. I know that's a big fat blanket statement, but I can tell you even in my own family, I've got family members who travel extensively and they are fairly well read and alive to the world. And then I have family members who don't ever plan to leave Mobile, Alabama.

DH: And they are quite happy where they are, and they don't have a problem with you doing what you're doing.
SM: Yep, exactly. And don't misunderstand, they are intelligent, well-read people, but their travel is nil. It's a big thing for them to go to DC. And so that's fine, that's their culture, but it does make a difference. And I think you have that tension in almost every nation of the world. I mean, I've talked to Scotsmen who say they are never going to London. What is that? A two-hour train ride or something? So, you have that element, but for the most part, the world is on the move. And just as in a lot of places you have a growing cultural gap between the wealthy and the non-wealthy, you are going to see a lot of daylight between those who have traveled and those who haven't, in terms of perspective.

It not only changes you, and you're delighted for it, it does distinguish you against those who are scared really to leave their burrows. I think more people are traveling; I think overall, travel is getting safer. But that still doesn't change the fact that you have this dividing line in most cultures of those who travel and those who don't. And it's as big as those who didn't get out of high school and those who have doctorates.

DH: Absolutely. Stephen, thank you so much. This has been fascinating. I appreciate your time.

Tony Wheeler

Tony Wheeler and his wife, Maureen, founded Lonely Planet in 1973. As you can probably guess, when I first met them for dinner in London, in 2013, we got along quite well. I was admittedly horribly intimidated, since I was running the company they had founded forty years prior, but they couldn't have been kinder.

What I learned as I got to know them is that travel is a way of life for the Wheelers. Since selling Lonely Planet to the BBC in 2007, their travel has only accelerated. Tony continues to see the world by any means possible, from a road trip across Asia in a vintage car to train rides across Mongolia. I caught up with the father of travel guides while we were both sitting on the phone overlooking the ocean—the Atlantic for me, the Pacific for Tony.

Daniel Houghton: How have you been? Where are you in the world right now?
Tony Wheeler: Very well. I'm in Sydney now.

DH: I'm down in the Florida Keys. On Marathon, right next to Key West.
TW: Nice. Let's do it!

DH: I'd love just a couple minutes on who you are, and what you want people to know about you. Then I'd love to hear what you've been up to recently, and where you've been.
TW: As you know, I traveled as a child because my father was working in various countries—Pakistan, the Bahamas, US, and

England. And back then countries like Iran and Afghanistan didn't get too many visitors, which inspired me to create Lonely Planet. I do still travel a lot, whether it's an archaeological trust or in the US with travel heritage firms. We've got a family trust that does fifty, sixty, seventy projects, mainly in Southeast Asia and East and West Africa. And I just go to places because I haven't been before, or there is an excuse to go back.

DH: Where have you been recently?

TW: For some reason, last year I went to quite a few countries I've never been to before. I traveled around what used to be Yugoslavia, which I enjoyed. The first time I went was back in the seventies, when it was one country, and now, of course, it's half a dozen countries.

I also did a little bit of travel last year in the sort of eastern extremes of Europe. I went to Moldova and to Belarus, Europe's nice dictatorship, as people like to say. I was also in Ukraine, and I was in a fascinating city down by Saint Petersburg.

The biggest trip I've done in the last few years was in 2017, so two years ago now. I joined a group of idiots ... we drove from Bangkok to London in old British sports cars, we had eight old MGs. We started off in Bangkok and drove up through Southeast Asia into China, joined the Silk Road, and spent four months driving all the way to London. It was a great trip. It was a trip that I guess in some ways is quite carefully planned, we knew where we were going. But really everybody was amazingly prepared.

We went through four to five -stans. Except Kyrgyzstan— that's the only -stan I haven't been to now. Everybody was friendly and welcoming everywhere. We just had a fantastic time. It could have been eight months instead of four months.

DH: How many of those cars broke down along the way? Or did you have pretty good luck?

TW: Oh, ha ha. Out of the eight cars, mine was actually the youngest, and they dated it from 1923. Some of them had more problems than others, but we had two or three people who were pretty good amateur mechanics, so we carried along well enough.

DH: That's great. When you think back early on, was it really just the fact that you had the opportunity to live in different countries when you were growing up with your dad that made you want to make this journey?

TW: No, not really. It's easy to say, "Well, did your traveling enthusiasm start from the fact that you've lived in different countries?" I mean it could have well done for me personally, but I've got a younger brother and a younger sister who didn't get bitten by the same travel bug. And you meet a lot of people who didn't have the opportunity to travel when they were young, who nevertheless become avid travelers. So I don't think the two things necessarily have to go together.

DH: You've been at this for a long time. How do you think travel has changed since you started?

TW: It's much simpler in many respects. You really just need to find out if you can fly there and if you can get a hotel. The internet works wonders—once upon a time, the only way of doing something was to turn up and see if they let you cross the border. On the other hand, I've just written the foreword to an academic study of over-tourism. Over-tourism is a word we use a lot these days in places like Barcelona and Amsterdam and Vienna. There are big question marks about how many tourists they can handle. But of course, there are many places in the world that suffer from under-tourism.

I think, for instance, in a place like India—I've traveled a lot over the years to India—at the Taj Mahal, there is not going to be a shortage of tourists. But India is a huge country, and you can go to a lot of places in India where they haven't seen a foreign tourist in the last twelve months.

So that's a country, in many respects, that is under-touristed, even if the raw numbers would say otherwise.

DH: Do you think travel is something that scares or intimidates people? And what would you say to people that are a little intimidated? My sense is that it's not just a financial burden that's preventing some people from traveling.
TW: Yeah. But you know, people are scared about all sorts of things. I always say, you can be run down by a drunk who drives away from a bar in your own hometown just as easily as you can have something go amiss in other parts of the world. Let's be honest, I traveled to the -stans two years ago and absolutely had no problems at all. Everybody was welcoming.

DH: One of the things that I was always very proud of with Lonely Planet is that we still worked hard to make sure every place we went to felt to us like a "Lonely Planet place." You can still open up the LP book and turn up to a place that you really wouldn't find online. Talk to me about how you shaped that aesthetic over the years, and what it means to you.
TW: You know, it started with the first traveling we did—on the hippie trail, when Iran and Afghanistan were wide open.

Pollution is a huge problem in the Kathmandu Valley. So we just started going down to Southeast Asia in the early seventies, when the Vietnam War was still winding down, so if you said "Southeast Asia" to an American, their first thought was the war.

It really wasn't till the early nineties that Laos, Vietnam, and Cambodia really reopened. The change in those countries—I was in both Cambodia and Vietnam in '91 and '92. And the changes from '92 until now are just amazing. Vietnam—you would not even recognize it today. So there have been huge changes. And at the end of the day, people go to these places and they still enjoy them. They still have a really good time there. That's the important element.

DH: What is your routine when you turn up to a new town? What's the first thing you do?
TW: I guess you check in to your hotel or wherever you're staying. And leave your bag and set out and walk. I think walking to places is how you immediately find out what it's like. I recently went to Azerbaijan, and I have never been there before, though I knew a little bit about it. Day one, when I arrived, the first thing I did was go out and walk around.

The next day I heard of these tours given by these local university students, and we got their perspective on their city. Only a week before that, I'd been in Cyprus, and again, it was a place I've never been to before. The interesting thing about Cyprus is that it's divided between Turkey and Greece. They actually put a border between the two parts of the island, and for many years you simply couldn't cross. But now you can. So by getting out and walking, you find out how things work.

DH: I know there are a million answers to this, but when you reflect back on all the places you've been, what have you learned about yourself?

TW: It's never the same the first time you travel without your parents. Getting a visa organized instead of having your parents doing it for you—it's an eye-opener, and a really good thing. I think someone could write a book about it. About young adults. How old were you when you first went somewhere else? Not with your parents. And lots of young people do go out more in very safe environments, and it's a really good way of starting. And even some younger people finish school and instead of going straight from school to college or further education, they take a year off and go somewhere. A lot of them come to Australia, and Australia is good. We speak the same language, but it's just different enough that you get a different experience. So I'm very enthusiastic about young people traveling; it's a real education. I probably learned more in that year off between school and university than in the next three years at university.

DH: Right.

TW: I have always liked that, once upon a time, when people thought about going somewhere they picked up a Lonely Planet book and thought, "You know, I could go there." And the young Chinese have always fascinated me because just a generation back, their parents didn't travel at all. They weren't allowed to leave the city where they were assigned to live. From not being able to leave the city to their offspring traveling all over the world. It's a huge change.

DH: That's really unbelievable to think about.

TW: I remember meeting a young Chinese guy a couple years ago. He and his wife set up a travel business based in Shanghai. They had about thirty or forty employees, tending to young people on adventurous trips.

And when he wanted to cross the border into Nepal, he didn't know what would happen, or how to do it. So he found the Lonely Planet guide in English. And he said to me, "I learned my English by reading Lonely Planet guides." And I think that is fantastic—that we affected not just people in the English-speaking world, but people outside of those regions.

DH: You, probably more than anyone else I've interviewed for this book, have built travel into a habit. And it's something that's part of your life that you do so often, year after year after year. Talk to me about the habit of that. And what would you tell people that have been afraid to take those big trips?

TW: Yeah, essentially I'm retired, so I've got the time and inclination. And in fact, I'd travel a lot more if I didn't have the family factor. But I'm not going to push it on other people. I'm looking across the bay here in Sydney, and only a few hundred yards away at a giant cruise ship. You know, I really don't have any interest in being on giant cruise ships. But I'm really glad. I'm glad a lot of people do, because it creates a lot more space for those of us who don't.

DH: Correct. I like to think about those people and go, "You know what, if that is their intro to travel—the one time they got off the boat or whatever—if that somehow sparks them into wanting to do more of that, I think that's wonderful."

TW: Yeah, I agree. And if they don't do any more, then that's fine as well.

DH: I know how much of a fan you are of cars, and I know you've taken more road trips than anyone I've ever met. If I said to you, "Okay, drive any car you want on any road in the world that you want," what kind of car would you pick? And where do you think you'd go?

TW: I did two trips across the US back in the nineties, more than twenty years ago, in an old American car, and I wanted to do it in a car from the fifties. Detroit's real era was the fifties. In those two trips, I managed to get to twenty-four of the lower forty-eight, so I did sort of half of America. I've still got about six states I haven't been to yet and I wouldn't mind just, you know, being in America and renting a car, driving to those six states. Three in the South and three up north. I haven't been to North Dakota yet.

DH: North Dakota is incredible.

TW: I would like to drive to the states I've never been to. It would be kind of fun to do it in an old car again, although I'm not terribly keen on keeping old cars going. If you haven't got a mechanic with you who knows how to fix them when they go wrong. It's different driving something new and reliable. I'll probably just rent a car.

DH: I think you'd really like North Dakota. I've been there a couple of times for vacation and it is stunningly beautiful. It's a very different type of beauty, almost alien.

TW: The other thing is I haven't done a really long train trip in the States. I was just thinking about doing Chicago to Seattle or

Chicago to San Francisco. You've got a week's stay. The articles I've read about it say that despite the fact that people can travel much cheaper and faster by getting a plane ticket, they still like the railway experience. So that would be a fun thing to do.

You know, I went on a European driving trip last year with some German friends. There was a young guy who was born in the old East Germany, and his family crossed over, when he was still a child, from east to west, just before the Berlin Wall went up. So, that was when you could just up and leave. It wasn't approved of, leaving nearly everything behind. But they did it. So we spent a couple of weeks with them, just driving around areas that he knew in the old East Germany. It was fascinating.

DH: I do have a rail question for you, which is, have you taken the railroad from Moscow to Beijing? What was that like?
TW: The Trans-Siberian—or in Beijing, it's the Trans-Mongolian. You go from Beijing up across Mongolia, and then you sort of link up with the Trans-Siberian, which starts in Russia. But you know, there's still another week from there to Moscow, so it's still quite a long trip. And you can do that trip in all sorts of different ways. If you do it on the cheap, you just get on the train, and you can take it to the next stop, when you get off and spend a day or so, then get on the train again, jump on another day. I must admit I did a very deluxe version of that. It was again German-organized, a train that a German group charters once a year.

DH: Oh wow. I feel like Maureen told me about that, right before you all went.
TW: A couple of places you get off the train, stay in a hotel, and then get back on the train. But it's effectively train all the way—it

was great. And, you know, you see a lot more of Russia, and you learn a lot more about Russia, away from the Moscows and Saint Petersburgs, the usual sort of tourist places. But around the same time, I forget, maybe it was a year later, I did another driving trip, in Pakistan. I wasn't driving. I had a driver and we used his car. And we went into Pakistan and we drove up to the border with China, and then got off and walked across the border and picked up a Chinese car on the other side and carried on up into Xinjiang Province. And in a way, it was a more interesting trip than the first. Both were fantastic trips, but I enjoyed that Karakoram Highway more.

And again, here we are in Pakistan, which has very few tourists. And yet our two weeks in Pakistan were just fantastic. We had a really good time, everybody was very friendly. We stayed in really interesting places. We saw lots of things—except other foreign tourists.

DH: Well, whenever you decide you're doing the road trip in the US—and it sounds like there's a couple of states left in the South—you give me a call, and we will make that happen.
TW: One, I think, is Minnesota. I don't have the list in front of me right now. I can't remember if it's Minnesota or not, you know, isn't it sort of its own country? Where Bob Dylan was born and grew up before he went to New York and became famous. It would be kind of interesting to do sort of a Bob Dylan pilgrimage and go to a couple of those places.

DH: I have to fly to Panama next week. Any tips?
TW: Panama City is an interesting city in all sorts of respects. The thing that really surprised me, though, is bird-watching. I'm not a

bird-watcher, but if you get an opportunity, go with someone who knows birds. The guy who took me around worked for Lonely Planet, and his line was that the Panama Canal was where the Rockies come down from North America and the Andes came up from South America. So you're in this zone of birds from the north and the south. The result is one of the most interesting bird habitats in the world. And I had a great day bird-watching—it was a real eye-opener.

BEFORE YOU GO

A Travel Checklist and Best Practices

I'll admit, I'm a bit of a travel nerd. I know, you could have guessed that, but I'm talking true nerd. I obsess over travel points and rewards programs. I check the type of aircraft before I book a flight, along with seat configuration. I almost always plan my entire trip around the airport I'm going to lay over in before a connecting flight.

I wanted to take the opportunity, now that I've essentially begged you to book a trip, to share some best practices you can use as a guide when you're traveling. These are not hard-and-fast rules, except for the first one. Make your own way through the world, and feel free to adjust these as necessary:

1. **Never check a bag.**
2. **See rule number one, don't break that.**
3. **Get to the airport early.** You can laugh, but most of the

travel fails in this book can be prevented entirely if you just get there an hour before you think you need to. Airports are fascinating places, even the bad ones. You can almost always find something fun to look at while walking around. There are endless amounts of food, drink, and shopping to keep you busy. If you're an airplane nerd like me, you will be in heaven.

4. **Be nice.** Seriously, to everyone. It's as effective as walking around handing out $20 bills to get what you want. Remember to smile.

5. **Ask questions.** To anyone and everyone. From the person you're sitting next to at the gate to the person running the gas station you walk past when you land. Some of the best advice I've ever gotten and the most unique opportunities I've experienced have come from these random encounters.

6. **Go for a walk whenever you land.** And be aware it may totally reroute your itinerary for the rest of your trip.

7. **Drink a lot of water.** You will see this written everywhere as a strategy to fight jet lag, and I'm here to tell you it works. Drink so much water that you're not even hungry. It will reward you endlessly throughout your trip if you keep it up.

8. **Carry at least $200 in local currency.** Not just for emergencies and safety situations. Having a little local cash in your pocket might unlock some unplanned experiences along the way.

9. **Call your friends and family.** Let them know you've arrived and then tell them exactly what they are missing out on. If FOMO is the silent driver of people booking

trips, I'm all for it. I do this almost every night with five to ten people back home. Don't worry about expensive international calls, just use FaceTime audio or the Android equivalent to call over the internet. Sharing your experiences with others is the best part.

10.   **Walk into a local bar with nothing planned for the night.** Order a drink, or not, up to you; but sit there and talk to people. Tell them where you're from, find out about their life, ask what's good to see and eat and drink in town.

11.   **Change your plans.** Either because once you've landed you found something better to do than you had planned, or you met someone to spend the day with. Do not be afraid to abandon your schedule when the right entertainment presents itself.

12.   **Pick up after yourself.** I shouldn't have to say this, but sometimes people's care for the world and our environment goes out the window when they travel. I get it, you're exhausted, maybe a little lost, but try to still be an example for others. One thing almost every interviewee told me is that they have always felt they were an ambassador for their home country.

13.   **Get lost.** This is not a joke. I would suggest taking your smartphone with a full battery before trying to get lost, but still, go for a long walk and make decisions on which way to go solely based on what looks interesting to you. When you're done, you can get out your phone and find your way home.

14.   **Make a friend.** And then stay in touch with them. I don't care if it's your cabdriver or the bartender at your hotel. I did this once with my cabdriver in London during a long

ride to Heathrow Airport, and now we've been friends for years. We have dinner together when I'm in town, and guess what? He doesn't charge to drive me to the airport anymore!

15. **Do something you would never do at home.** Push yourself outside your comfort zone. This could be eating a crazy food you've never tried before or bungee jumping off the bridge where it was invented in New Zealand. Travel is all about new experiences, and if you make it all the way there to not try anything new, you're missing the best parts.

16. **Get a good travel rewards credit card.** Now that you're hooked on travel, you need to be taking full advantage of the financial gain achieved by booking travel through the right credit card and banking the points for your next trip. It can be a bit of a hassle to get going, but if you don't play the points game, you're essentially letting free money burn. These cards are lucrative and, honestly, essential for maximizing what you can afford. I've been doing this successfully for years, and I have paid actual money for fewer than five flights in the last decade and a million miles of travel. I can't tell you which one's the best, but the Points Guy (www.pointsguy.com) can.

17. **Spend time thinking about life back home while you're on the road.** Okay, now I'm probably confusing you, but I'm serious. Once you've been out of your element for a few days exploring your new destination, sit down over a beer one night and think through your life back home. What have you learned on this trip about yourself or your life at home that you can change or want to improve? Take out a piece of paper and write it all down. They can be good,

bad, or ugly observations, but no matter what, I promise you will enjoy this exercise.

18. **Give back to the local community.** It doesn't matter if this is dropping the last $20 of local currency into a tip jar before you take off or, if you have the time, volunteering somewhere. Spending time with the locals is one of the most rewarding parts of exploring new destinations.

19. **Document everything.** Take pictures, of everything. Not so much that you forget to live in the moment, of course, but make sure you get some memories for when you're home. Record the sound of traffic on your phone, record local bands you hear play or conversations you have (with permission, of course). These small acts will reward you for the rest of your life when you reflect back on your trip and want to remember what it was like to be there. It will also inspire you to get out your suitcase again!